A CO-WORKER'S CRUSH

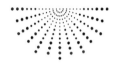

PIPER RAYNE

Cover Photo: Wander Aguiar Photography

Cover Design: By Hang Le

1st Line Editor: Joy Editing

2nd Line Editor: My Brother's Editor

Proofreader: Shawna Gavas, Behind The Writer

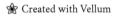 Created with Vellum

ABOUT A CO-WORKER'S CRUSH

Three tattoo guns.
Five motorcycle tires.
Countless T-shirts.

That's what I lost before I realized nothing good comes from dating my co-workers.

Usually, I don't have much self-control. So, the fact that Frankie Grant is a hot, talented tattoo artist means it's a damn miracle she hasn't already been in my bed. But nothing can happen between us because Frankie comes with Jolie, her young daughter, and a crap load of baggage from her ex. And those are two things I never entertain.

Anyone who knows me—the screwed up foster kid from the wrong side of the tracks—knows I'm not the guy you take home to meet your parents, let alone your kid. But I also know what it's like not to have parents, so things get complicated when Jolie asks me to be her daddy.

I might as well just slash my own tires.

A CO-WORKER'S CRUSH

CHAPTER ONE

Jax

*P*sychologists have nothing on tattoo artists. We might not hold the fancy degree, but we hear people's life stories all the time. The difference is that we brand them with ink to help them remember whatever lesson or experience they're intent on carrying with them. It's a lot of pressure. Take my most recent client—who's a babbler to the nth degree.

"And then bam, headlights were shining right in my face." The guy springs up as though I need a reenactment of his near-death experience.

"Sit down. Unless you want me to fuck up your tattoo," I say, wiping the outline of the stencil off his skin since he moved.

He lies back down on my table. "So that's why I'm here— to remember that feeling when I thought my life was over."

He flings his head to move his red hair that's falling down over his eyes. "Have you ever had one of those experiences?"

I glance at Dylan and he smirks, wiping the skin of his client, who came in for a killer piece he had Dylan draw. Those are the best clients—the ones who let you ink their skin with your art.

"All the damn time." I wipe the area I'm going to be working on.

Dylan chuckles, but I don't look at him again. We grew up in a shitty neighborhood, and since we're both foster kids, we never put much weight in the whole one life analogy.

"I'm sure. Look at you." The kid stares at my full sleeve tatted arm. "You probably ride a motorcycle."

I nod, and he groans.

"Without a helmet?"

I click my tongue on the roof of my mouth to say no. "Nope. There was a time I was stupid enough to do that, but I've seen too much shit. People who don't get up off the concrete." I place the stencil on his skin, and he flinches. This is going to be torture for us both. "You gotta sit still."

"And you've probably skipped school? Smoked and not just cigarettes, right?"

I glance over my shoulder at Dylan. He's biting his lip so hard it's gonna bleed.

"And girls? You probably had two chicks willing to do you at the same time." The kid groans. "That's never gonna happen for me."

Frankie, my co-worker, gags. "He's not an idol to look up to, kid."

I give her a big toothy smile and she flips me off. We have a love-hate relationship, but it's heavy on the hate. She'd never admit it, but her life would be boring without me in it. God knows the woman needs a few laughs in her life. Not that she finds much humor in what I say.

"You gotta understand where I'm coming from," my client says. "I was captain of the chess team, valedictorian of my class, got one date to the prom—but that was with my neighbor who went to an all-girls' school because she felt sorry for me. Went to my dad's alma mater, majored in business just like him, pledged his fraternity. It wasn't the cool keg party fraternity—mine held study sessions and quiz nights."

The kid has no idea the life he was granted. I'm pretty sure he had Christmas presents every year, birthdays that were celebrated—not to mention parents who took pictures of him before he went to prom, who gushed over his graduation, and who paid for all his shit. Long ago, I would have told this kid to be grateful for what he has, but I'm over it now.

"Sucks," I agree with him because it's just easier.

"I know, right? Tell me, how many chicks do you get?"

Dylan loses his fight and laughs. Frankie groans again. Lyle's ears perk up. He's an aspiring tattoo artist, and I'm one hundred percent sure he's picked this profession to try to get girls.

I shrug. "Depends on the night."

"Just so you know, kid, he isn't getting any women in his bed at the moment." Frankie lets out an evil laugh.

We're still on that bet about how long I can go without getting laid. Was the bet stupid? Hell yes, but she started it. And I'm proud to say that though my balls are blue as a Smurf and my left palm is calloused beyond belief, I still haven't had sex yet.

"Why?" The kid flings his head back again to get the red strands out of his vision.

I point at him in warning. "I'm gonna put it in a ponytail if you don't stop."

"I have a clip." Frankie waves Lyle over from the front

desk. He does as she says because he's so desperate he'd even try to nail Frankie. Hate to break it to the kid, but he could never handle Frankie. "Top drawer, it's Jolie's."

Lyle brings the clip over and pushes the kid's hair away before sticking a Paw Patrol barrette in his hair.

"This is embarrassing as hell," my client mumbles.

"Either that or I mess up the tattoo." I wait for him to argue, but he doesn't.

So I prepare my ink and machine, ready to get this tattoo started. Hopefully with the first prick of the needle, the kid shuts up and I'll get in my zone. If he passes out, I'm done.

"So why haven't you had sex?" he asks.

Frankie laughs. "Go ahead and tell your little wannabe mini-me why."

"She bet me I couldn't go a week." I nod in Frankie's direction.

"And what do you get if you win?" the kid asks.

I glance at Frankie, and she stops tattooing her girl to look at me. "Just the satisfaction that she was wrong."

"So when is the week up?" he asks.

"It was over weeks ago," Dylan interjects. "I tried to tell Frankie that Jax doesn't mess around with bets. So now we all have to deal with his cranky-ass attitude."

As embarrassing as it is, he's right. I'm doing it to prove a point, but at this point, I'm not even sure who or what for. And I am on edge. More than I'm willing to admit. Not that I'm a womanizing whore, but knowing all prospects are off the table does not make me a happy man.

"Why are you still doing it?" The kid tries to turn his head to see Frankie.

Her head is down, concentrating on the girl's neck she's tattooing. I'm going to have to decide when I'll finally give in. But so far, it just hasn't felt like the right time.

"Because Jax takes everything to the umpteenth degree," Dylan says.

"We could wager again?" I offer.

Frankie looks at me from the corner of her eye as she dips her needle in the ink. "You like having blue balls, huh?"

"No blue balls," I lie. "In fact, you star in my highlight reel every night."

"Highlight would mean you've had sex with her?" The kid tries again to look at Frankie as though he wants to picture the two of us.

"I assure you, kid, I would never be caught in bed with Jax."

"That's perfect because I'm not an 'in bed' kind of guy." I grin at her.

She huffs and goes back to working on her client.

"Can we please stop talking about this? Lyle, turn up the music," Dylan orders.

"Yeah, because you don't know how to treat a woman with respect," Frankie says.

I should leave this topic be, but if I did, I wouldn't be Jax Owens. "No woman wants to be fucked in a respectable way."

Her groan turns into a growl and I smile at my client, having gotten the exact reaction out of her that I wanted. Yes, might as well enroll me back in the seventh grade for how I love to antagonize her.

"Turn up the damn music, Lyle." Dylan's voice sounds pained.

I buzz the needle on my client's skin—finally—and although he closes his eyes, he surprises me by taking the pain. If only I could get the idea of fucking Frankie out of my head now. I swear I can almost feel her slim hips under my hands as I drill inside her, watching her hatred for me dissolve into lust. I wasn't lying about her being in my reel. It might be imaginary, but she's my go-to lately and I think it's because of the bet. Which probably means I need to put an end to the bet, because I never screw my co-workers. Ever.

A half-hour later, I finish his tattoo. It's binary code for "no risk no gain" which is a new one for me. He put it on the inside of his bicep, so I give him props for that. I've seen other men tear up when I tattoo that area.

Once I'm done, he walks to the mirror. This is my favorite part of my job—seeing the immediate reaction to the tattoo.

His eyes light up and I think he might be a little proud of himself too. "I love it."

"Let's go over care instructions." I take off my gloves and throw them away.

He doesn't turn away from the mirror. The kid is speech-less for the first time since he walked in here. I lean back in my chair and find myself smiling at him like a proud father.

Still looking in the mirror, he says, "I know you don't get it, but all my life, it's like I've been stuck in this box. All my parents' expectations, teacher expectations, peer expectations. After that truck almost ran me over, it was like *bam*, I thought I'm going to die, and I haven't done one thing *I* truly wanted in this life."

The tattoo needles behind me quiet. I'm sure if I looked back, I'd see Dylan and Frankie listening to his speech.

"This is the first step of my new life. So many things I've put on the back burner and thought 'one day.' Well, that day is now." He looks at the floor for a second then looks back up. "I'm sure none of you understand because you're the kind of people who have done what you wanted your entire life. You didn't let anyone put you in a two-by-two box, shoving you back down every time you spoke up."

I glance over my shoulder, and Dylan raises his eyebrows. The kid is right on one hand—no one was going to tell me what to do—but everyone has things they say they're going to do one day and keep putting off.

"Not necessarily true," I say.

He points at Dylan and me. "Look at you guys. You're the epitome of tough guys."

Frankie laughs. "I'm going to give you one piece of advice." I hear the snap of her gloves being taken off, which means she must be done with her client as well.

Frankie and her client walk over to the kid, and Frankie holds the mirror in front of her client's face so she can see the tattoo on the back of her neck. The kid stares at the girl and I already know how this is going to turn out.

Frankie interrupts before he can say anything. "Outward appearance has nothing to do with being tough. You think because they have tattoos and give off that 'I don't give a shit' attitude that they're not afraid of things? They are. Being the only female working in this tattoo parlor, I'm here to tell you, it's not muscle and tattoos that make someone tough. It's perseverance, taking the shit life throws at you and not letting it tear you down. Being a good person in spite of it all."

He nods, but I'm not sure he understands what Frankie is saying. I heard her loud and clear though.

"Do you want to go out with me?" he asks the girl without any preamble.

I wince because though I love this kid's "take life by the horns" outlook, his delivery could use some work. I don't want to see his newfound attitude about life deteriorate.

"Sure. But." She takes the clip out of his hair and hands it to Frankie.

"Thanks." The kid's cheeks grow redder than they already are.

"That's better," she says and smiles.

Even Frankie turns around and raises her eyebrows in surprise as they walk out of the parlor together after paying.

"Maybe we should start a board with love matches made here," Lyle says.

No one says anything. I can't speak for my co-workers, but the kid got me thinking about the one thing I've been putting on the back burner ever since I attended the testicular cancer awareness ball with my friends and heard them talk about how it can be genetic.

When I was younger, I never put too much thought into my future, but it's time I face my biggest fear—finding my birth parents.

CHAPTER TWO

Frankie

*W*hen I walk in after my late shift, Sandy is asleep on the chair, the remote in her blanket-covered lap, so I slowly shut the door and tiptoe across the room.

As I place my purse on the kitchen table, my gut twists when I spot the Styrofoam cup from Nikki's Gyros. Only one person brings that food in this house. Instead of nudging Sandy awake, I walk down the hall and peek into Jolie's room.

Her rainbow nightlight's glow allows me to see that she's fast asleep with the polar bear stuffed animal snug under her arm. Jax won it for her from one of those crane games at Pizza Pies the last time we all went.

I shut the door and walk quietly back down the hall. Sandy is folding the blanket when I reach the living room.

"You can spend the night." I always offer and she always declines.

"No. I'm good."

I pick up the Styrofoam cup and she sighs, which means it wasn't her who went there. She had a visitor while I was at work.

"He came for about five minutes and left. Jolie cried herself to sleep again." Sandy shakes her head.

She carries the burden of my ex's addiction. She shouldn't. She's always been there for him, but after the death of his father, Michael spun out of control. Sandy was grieving herself. It was a tornado of things that never fully landed back in their original spot.

I throw away the cup like I'd like to throw him out.

"Was he here for money?" I ask.

"I think so, but he never did have the nerve to ask after Jolie cornered him about Christmas coming up and asking where he was at Thanksgiving." She lingers, putting on her coat and retrieving her keys out of her purse. "Frankie." There's a hitch in her tone that's not usually there. "I don't think he wanted the money for drugs though."

I perk up, hoping that maybe he finally wants help. Not that we'll ever get back together, but I would like Jolie to have a father in her life. "Oh?"

"He's... leaving."

"What?" I jerk back.

She puts up her hand up to stop me from overreacting. "He said after Christmas. That his friends are going west."

"And what about Jolie?" I pace the front room, unable to process how he can treat his little girl with such little regard. All she wants is him. She doesn't care that he's a low-life druggie who hits women. All she sees is her father.

"I know. I said that, but you know him. He thinks he's no good for her."

"I think that's an excuse," I say, too meanly to the woman who bore him. I've always tried to bite my tongue when we talk about Michael. I try to be sensitive to the fact that she's his mother, not to mention the help she gives me with Jolie can't be replaced.

"I'm not sure it is, but regardless, I think we have to prepare Jolie."

"I think he's already been doing that by popping in and out of her life the past year." Ever since I left him and got my own apartment, he makes and breaks promises all the time.

She nods and sighs.

"Sandy, you have to stop feeling responsible."

"He's my son. Of course I feel like I did something wrong for him to turn out like this. And I wish every night he could just see the light, but now with this move… it kills me to say this, but maybe it's for the best."

Is she really suggesting that no dad is what's best for Jolie? But after a few seconds, my shoulders sag because she's right. At this point, Jolie grieves after every one of his sporadic visits. She's hurt and sad and can't understand why she's not good enough for her dad. I wanted to spare her the feeling of unwantedness that I endured after my dad left us and never returned, but Sandy's right—she's better off without Michael.

"Is he planning on telling me?" I ask.

She shakes her head.

"That means I have to go for sole custody now. I can't allow him to leave and possibly take her God knows where. What if he finds a lawyer and a sympathetic judge somewhere and he gets custody, only to abandon her because he wasn't clean? Jolie needs stability."

She nods. "That's why I'm telling you."

I cross the room and hug the woman who's growing frailer by the day. I've asked her to move in with us on numerous occasions, but she shoots me down every damn time.

"Thank you… for everything," I manage to get out past the ball of emotion clogging my throat.

She pats my back. "You girls are my family. I'm so s—"

I push her back by the shoulders and set my gaze on her. "Do not apologize for him."

She waits a moment. We both know she wants to say it. "I should go. So I'll pick her up after preschool tomorrow, then I'm taking her to see that movie, remember?"

"Thanks. One day I'm going to pay you back for this."

She laughs. "Just visit me in the old folks' home, okay? I don't want to be one of those sad people they wheel in front of the nurses' station to watch everyone who comes there to see other people."

I laugh because she'll never see the inside of an old folks' home if it's up to me. "Deal."

She smiles and squeezes my hand before she leaves. "You're so strong, you amaze me."

I shake my head. People tell me I'm strong—but for what? Being a single mother? What choice do I have? My strength comes from not having any other option. But my life begins and ends with that little girl, and no man will ever come between that.

"You're strong," I say to her.

She laughs and opens the door. "Now lock up after I leave."

"Text me when you get home, okay?"

She nods and I wait until she's at the elevator before I shut my door and lock it. Then I watch her walk along the sidewalk and get in her car. I really hate having her leave so late at night to head home. It's not going to work much longer.

"Mommy?" Jolie says, walking in from the hall.

"Hey, sweet girl." I open up my arms and she walks into my embrace. I pick her up and she rests her head on my shoulder.

"Daddy came," she says.

"I heard."

"Him and Grandma were yelling."

I kiss her forehead. I had a feeling. Although I'm fairly sure the screaming was him, not Sandy. I can't blame her if she did yell. I've lost my cool with him more than once.

"Come on, let's go to bed." I shut off all the lights, grab my phone out of my purse, and head down the hall.

"Can I sleep with you tonight?" she asks.

"Sure thing, kiddo." I turn off her nightlight and she reaches for the polar bear.

I sigh because part of me hates that Jax Owens has wormed his way into my daughter's heart. Sometimes I question why he's taken such an active role in my daughter's life, but then it's probably my own fault. Jolie's at Ink Envy so much, he didn't have much choice.

She snuggles into my bed, and I strip down, not bothering to brush my teeth or wash my face. Some days are too exhausting. Maybe I'll regret it when I'm fifty, but right now, I just want my head on the pillow.

Jolie cuddles into me, and I wrap my arm around her and squeeze her tightly because I know things might get really messy once I file for custody. Michael might be leaving Cliffton Heights and the east coast altogether, but me filing paperwork for sole parental rights will infuriate him. Even though he doesn't want us, he's always believed that he owns us.

THE NEXT MORNING, I do my research and get the name of a family lawyer a friend of a friend used to get sole custody of her children. When I call to make an appointment, I find out the lawyer had two cancelations, so I pick the appointment time that allows me to stop by after work.

All I can think of during my shift is what's going to happen. I imagine Michael's reaction after the papers are served. He's bound to confront me. Maybe I should take Jolie and hole us up in a hotel. But I try not to uproot her too much. She's already had so many changes in her young life.

"What do you think, Spark Plug?" Jax asks from his chair. He's currently leaned into a chair with his boots crossed up on his station, sketching in his journal.

"About what?" I work on my own sketch for my client who's scheduled to arrive in about five minutes.

Dylan walks over and squeezes my shoulder. "What's with you today? You don't seem all there."

He's the best boss I could ever have. I know that even his friends would let Jolie and me stay at their apartments. Which makes me feel slightly better if I decide to go that route after serving Michael.

"Nothing, just preoccupied. What did you say?" I ask, fixing the shading on my sketch.

"Christmas?" Dylan fills me in.

"Sure. Do you mind if I invite Sandy?"

Jax watches me from the corner of his eye. I hate how he knows so much about my life, but I know nothing about his.

"Jackass skipping the holidays this year?" Jax asks.

I stiffen. "I'm not sure, but I know she'd rather be with Jolie than alone."

His feet drop to the floor and he tosses the journal on his table. "Of course, who wouldn't? I gotta take a piss."

He disappears down the hall to the bathroom. I always find it strange how Jax can hate a person he's never met.

Michael won't come into Ink Envy—I think he's afraid of what my co-workers might do or say to him if he did.

"Rian wants to have it at our place. She's got a lot of shit to get done. So if you need a place to stay, I'm sure she'd love the extra help," Dylan says while walking by me to the front counter. The man knows me well.

"I'll see. Jolie would love it."

Dylan chuckles, grabbing the appointment book. "So would Rian. She loves baking with Jolie, and she has certain Christmas cookies she wants to bake at the house instead of Sweet Infusion because they're supposed to be *homemade*. Not sure what the location of baking has to do with it."

"But you're not going to argue with her, am I right?"

He laughs. "Hell no. What I'm saying is that you'd be saving me if you wanted to stay a few days."

We both know Dylan is asking because Michael might show up at my place unannounced like he usually does, and I'm not interested in ruining Jolie's Christmas. "Thanks."

He nods. "I'll be in the back if you need me."

He leaves and Jax returns, sighing as he sits back down. "You shouldn't have to hide out."

Luckily, my client walks in before I cry and tell Jax all my problems. I have no idea how I hate him so much, but at the same time, he's like a therapist to me. I could see him just sitting there, letting me unload it all on him.

"Mind your own business." I stand to greet my client. "Hey, I was just finishing up your sketch."

I purposely don't look at Jax for fear I'll crumble.

After my shift, I get in my car, and head to the opposite side of town. The side of Cliffton Heights where the country club is—and the fancy lawyer's office.

I open up the door, give them my name, and sit in the waiting area. My knee bounces and I feel sick to my stomach. Maybe I should just go.

15

The door of the office opens, and for a moment, I consider bolting. If Michael leaves town, what does it matter whether I have custody or not? But this has been a long time coming and I can't allow him to treat Jolie like the Holiday Inn, so I stay seated in my chair.

But when the person comes into the room, his presence demanding as always, my stomach sinks. What the hell is Jax doing in a family law office?

CHAPTER THREE

Jax

*W*hen I see Frankie sitting in the office, I debate whether I should rush out. Maybe she won't see me or know I was here. But our eyes lock and there's no escaping this, so I might as well own my decision.

"Frankie." I nod at her and head over to the receptionist.

She looks like a mom, maybe even a young grandma. I wonder if the lawyer does that on purpose, to make his clients comfortable.

"Jax Owens," I tell her.

She types in my name and hands me a clipboard. "Great, you're a little early, but he'll be with you shortly."

I nod and grab a mint before sitting down next to Frankie. Might as well spend my time annoying her. It is one of my favorite pastimes after all.

"What are you doing here?" she asks the minute I pop the mint in my mouth.

I slide it around with my tongue. "I'm here to see about adopting a kid."

She doesn't believe my bullshit, so she stares blankly, and I chuckle.

"Why are you here?" I knock shoulders with her.

"I asked you first." She shuts the magazine she wasn't really reading and puts it on the table before crossing her arms, causing the fabric of her shirt to gape across her chest.

As horrible as it is, I want to see Frankie's tits. They aren't huge, but they're shapely and she rarely wears anything that gives a glimpse of cleavage. That's probably why I want to see them. Just mere curiosity.

"I'm here to see if I can find my birth parents."

Her smirk vanishes and regret over sharing that with her eats at me. I haven't told anyone. I'm not sure why I didn't just lie. But why else would I be in a family lawyer's office? I think my ability to lie has faded since returning to Cliffton Heights.

"Oh." Based on her tone, she clearly has an opinion on the matter.

"Oh what?"

"I just figured you didn't really care about your birth parents. Like once they left you, they were dead to you."

I school my surprise. She either knows me too well or I'm that transparent. "You're right. They are dead to me, but you know that keynote speaker at the testicular cancer fundraiser Dylan and Rian dragged us to?"

She nods.

"He said it was hereditary. So now I wanna know if I'm gonna lose a ball."

"Oh, so just for the medical background information?"

"That's what I said. If my dick is in danger, I want to know."

That's not completely it. I mean, I do want to know if

there's something I should be concerned about or on the lookout for. What if I come from one of those families where no male has survived past fifty or something?

"Do you have any information about your birth parents?" she asks.

This might be the first *real* conversation I've ever had with Frankie. I mean, I overhear her telling Dylan stuff and I'll input my two cents, but as far as her finding out anything about me, I've remained tight-lipped. "Not really. I have a birth certificate with no father's name and most likely a fake mother's name."

Her lips tip down.

Time to steer this conversation in another direction. "Your turn."

"I want sole custody of Jolie. Rumor is Michael's leaving for the west coast, and I don't want him trying for joint custody and dragging Jolie across the country."

"About damn time." I've always wondered why she lets her douche of an ex be involved in either of their lives.

She nods, and I glance at her finger picking the skin away from her thumbnail.

"You're doing the right thing," I assure her.

"I know. I do. It's just that she's his daughter. He's her dad."

"He's a shit dad."

"But still her dad. Look at you. You're trying to find your birth parents."

"Not for some happy reunion. Strictly for medical information."

She nods. "Okay, but you're seeking them out. It goes to show that sometimes things leave gaping wounds that never get filled."

"Don't typecast me as some wounded foster kid. I made

19

peace with my upbringing a long time ago." There's bitterness in my tone that contradicts my words.

Frankie's not a moron. I'm not sure I've ever met a foster kid who got over it completely. Although Dylan's doing a bang-up job with Rian at the moment.

"I'm not," Frankie says. "I'm just saying, no matter the person he is, he's still her father. And he's never touched her."

"Yeah, but how long before he does? The first time she talks back to him?" I clench my fists, thinking about him raising his hands at Jolie.

"I'm not sure he ever would, but you're probably right."

"Don't forget it. Did he show any interest in his daughter when you two were together?" I'm prying and I should probably stop. Frankie's home life is more normal than abnormal to me because the only person I've ever known—before moving here—who had both parents who loved them was Knox.

"Not really. He's never been the best dad."

"Frankie, let's take off the rose-colored sunglasses for a moment. He used to hurt you. He used to hit you." I grit my teeth when I think about someone taking their hands to her.

She squeezes her eyes shut and nods. I don't like that I'm causing her pain, but she needs to hear the truth.

"Maybe not now, but one day he's going to do that to her."

"Frankie Grant," the receptionist calls from an ajar door across the way.

"Do you want me to go in with you?" I ask.

She rises from the chair and clutches one hand in the other. "No, I've got this."

I sit back in the chair and pick up a magazine. That's the thing about Frankie—she doesn't think she needs anyone, but one day she's going to find out how badly she does.

———

FRANKIE COMES out from her appointment and heads to the reception desk to make her next one while I get called in.

"Hey, wait for me?" I ask her. She's finished work, and she was talking earlier about Sandy taking Jolie to the movies, so I know she has time.

"Why?"

The assistant's eyes peer up from her computer at me.

"Just wait."

"What gives?" Frankie asks.

We don't have a friendly relationship. I'm pretty sure she hates me. But I have to think that what she's doing is hard and what I'm about to is as well. Maybe she could use someone to listen.

"Just a cup of coffee."

She sighs. "I'd rather take a shot."

"Deal."

I don't wait for her to argue further, walking through the door and following the woman who called my name. She knocks and opens the door, introducing me to Mr. Holder.

He holds out his hand over his desk and I shake it. The assistant closes the door when she leaves. I notice the box of Kleenex on the desk and the trash can filled with used tissues.

"What brings you in, Mr. Owens?"

"Jax, please," I say.

He nods and waits with his fingers weaved together over the desk.

"I was put into foster care and I'd like to find my birth parents."

He nods. "Okay. What kind of information do you have?" I hand over my birth certificate, and he glances at it. "No father's name, but you do have the name of your mother." I nod and he sets down the paperwork. "I have a partner who investigates these cases. I'm not sure what he'll find out, but we can try. May I ask what you're looking for by reuniting with them?"

I lean back in the chair and rest my ankle on my knee. "Oh, I don't want a reunion. I just want the health information. I don't want to meet either of them if you happen to find them."

He leans back in his big fancy chair. "Okay. Well, that might be easier, but I want to warn you, this is opening Pandora's Box. You might not want to reunite, but I've seen it where the party who didn't initiate the search does. Are you prepared for that?"

I lean forward, my foot falling to the floor. "If I hire you, you're my lawyer, right? You can't give out information about me."

"Yes, but oftentimes they find you once that door is opened."

"Let's just make this clear. I don't want either of them to know one thing about me. I just want my family medical history. That's it."

He picks up my birth certificate. "Let me see where we get with this and I'll be in touch. Unless you want a second opinion?"

"No, I heard you were the best?" I say it like a question.

He nods. "You heard right."

His confirmation solidifies that I hired the right guy. You have to be an arrogant fucker to be a lawyer. "Then what do I owe for your retainer?"

He tells me, and I pull my checkbook from my leather jacket. My pen stops at the total amount. "The woman who was here before me… Frankie Grant? Did she hire you?"

"You know that's privileged information. You'll have to talk to her about that."

I like this guy already. I double the amount of my check, thinking a retainer is a retainer to this guy.

"Here." I tear the check out of my book and slide it to him. "I'm paying both retainer fees. If she paid you, rip up the check."

"But—"

"But nothing. It's money."

"I can't let you do that." He looks at me from under his eyebrows.

"Listen, Frankie is a single mom, and she shouldn't have to worry about paying her rent or stealing money from her kid's college fund because her ex can't get his shit together. Just take it."

He nods and accepts the check before pulling another one from his drawer and ripping it up. "I can't tell you anything even if you are paying the bills."

Man, Mr. Holder is the shit. I'd hire him again if I didn't already. "Good. I just want her to win."

"Well, with family cases—" He's quick to stop talking.

I stand and hold my hand out over the desk. "So you'll be in touch?"

Holder rises to his feet and shakes my hand. "Yes. I'll forward this on today."

"Thanks."

I leave his office to find Frankie waiting for me, much to my surprise. I make a follow-up appointment for the next week, then I open the door, waiting for Frankie to walk through first.

"And to what do I owe this gentlemanly behavior?" she asks.

"Because we're both dealing with shitty things, so we're going to commiserate together."

"I should get home. I have to do laundry."

I shake my head. "Your dirty panties can wait."

"They really can't. And can you not be so crass?"

We walk into the elevator, where I press the ground floor

button and the doors shut. "I promise, you'd love this crass mouth in bed."

She shakes her head. "Does that really work on most women?" The doors open and she walks out.

"You'd be surprised. Sometimes I don't even have to talk at all."

She rolls her eyes right before pushing through the circular doors. "Ew."

Once we're on the streets of Cliffton Heights, I figure the best idea will be to drive home and walk to the bar because I'm not going to drink and drive. "Meet me at the Velvet Bar?"

She huffs, walking toward her car.

"Come on, you need a fun night. Jolie's with Sandy. And I promise not to ruin your only clean pair of panties." I wink.

She huffs but giggles. "Fine. One drink."

She slides into her car, and I straddle my bike. As I ride through the streets to park at my apartment and walk down to Velvet Bar, I wonder why I care so much about Frankie's predicament. I could easily chalk it up to all the shit I saw as a foster kid. The physical abuse I saw not just against women, but men too. Some women use those nails like claws. At some point while growing up, I started protecting the younger kids like it was ingrained in me. Might be the only good quality that came from being passed around like a joint.

Frankie isn't one to ever ask for help, so I'm offering before she has to ask. I swear, one of these days, playing savior is going to bite me in the ass.

CHAPTER FOUR

Frankie

*A*fter driving home and parking, I sat in my car for over ten minutes, second-guessing whether I should meet Jax or not. It's weird that he even offered for me to meet him for a drink.

I should just go home, do laundry, and wait for Sandy to come back with Jolie. But when is the last time I went out without Jolie? And a little adult time doesn't sound so bad—even if it's with Jax. Maybe the two of us can find some sort of tenuous friendship. Plus, I could use a drink after hearing how much Mr. Holder's retainer is.

It's a quick walk over and I open the doors of the Velvet Bar. The walls are lined with red velvet, the furniture all black leather, and the place is dimly lit. After the doors close and my eyes acclimate to the darkness of the bar, I spot Jax in a booth near the back.

"One drink," I murmur to myself while I make my way over to him.

"About time, Spark Plug. Did you rush home and shave your legs just in case you got lucky tonight?"

That friends idea goes right out the window. "Are you suggesting *you'd* get lucky? That I'd be the woman who breaks your resolve?" Somehow, I avoid rolling my eyes.

"My balls are chained up."

The waitress comes by and drops off two shots.

"Shots?" I raise an eyebrow.

"Yes, we're celebrating like you already won." Jax grins.

"Could I get a water and a martini?" I ask the waitress.

She nods, and when I turn back to the table, Jax has his shot glass in the air. "Let's toast."

"What are we toasting to and why are you being so nice? I'm scared."

He chuckles. "I am a nice guy if you don't typecast me within minutes of meeting me."

I'd never admit to him that he's a nice guy when it comes to Jolie. With her, he's almost sweet. But he's still the same guy I thought he was the first day he started at Ink Envy. His ability to maintain his celibacy for a while doesn't change that.

I raise my shot glass.

"To you getting sole custody of Jolie."

"And you finding your birth parents," I add.

"Only their information, but yes." We clink the glasses together and down the shots.

The waitress comes by with my martini and Jax's whiskey. He's usually a beer drinker when we're out with everyone. I wonder what the lawyer told him.

We sit in silence, listening to sexy lounge music as I sip my martini.

"So want to talk about the lawyer and what he said?" he asks me.

I shake my head, tears already threatening to fall. I knew what my reality was when I decided to pursue sole custody, but Holder's confirmation just set it in cement.

"Come on."

I stop twirling the stem of my glass and set my eyes on him. "What is this?"

His forehead wrinkles. "What's what?"

"This." I wave my finger between us. "We're not really friends. I know we coexist at work and you do things for Jolie—which I do appreciate—but we hate one another."

"I don't hate you." He seems surprised that I would think that.

I blow out a breath. "Why are we having a drink?" I could be at home with a box of Kleenex and a carton of ice cream.

"Because I know this is tough on you and I'm not exactly an open book, so you're the only one who knows what I'm doing. I figure we'd drink to the shitty situations we're in. That's all." He shrugs.

I nod. "Okay."

"Plus you look sad, and for some damn reason, I hate when people are sad."

I shake my head at him.

Jax adds, "I came late to the group. Wanna tell me about him?"

"Who?" I ask, already knowing who he's talking about.

"The ex? The douche? The asshole? Whatever you'd like to call him."

I twirl the stem of my glass then sip my drink, needing the burn of the gin down my throat. "He's an addict, and when he uses, he gets angry. When he gets angry, he hits. Rumor from Sandy is that he's moving west, so I want to get this over with before he goes."

There, I just told him all of it without shedding one tear.

"It's a good idea. You don't want him coming back to Jolie in a year or two with his own demands. Better to get it sorted now. I've been in the system and seen enough shit to know that biology holds more weight than someone's treatment of their kid."

"It must have been hard being a foster kid."

He downs a big gulp of his drink. "Want another shot?"

I shake my head. "You're not taking advantage of me tonight."

He raises his hands and orders two more shots anyway. "I'm pretty sure I could strip down naked and you wouldn't react. You're the only woman in Cliffton Heights who I repulse apparently."

I'd never admit it to him, but he's wrong. I notice a lot about Jax. I'm not sure any girl would find him unattractive. He's tall with lean muscles and tatted-up with a chip on his shoulder. He rides a motorcycle. Hell, he's the epitome of every dirty dream I have. But guys like him aren't stepfathers. He's sweet to Jolie, but if push came to shove, he wouldn't want a little girl getting in the way of what he wants to do.

Two more shots land on the table, and Jax holds one up. "To a platonic relationship."

I clink and down the shot, the burn coating my throat in a glorious way.

My phone dings and I pull it out of my purse.

Sandy: *The movie is just starting. I promised her ice cream after. I'll let you know.*

Me: *Thanks Sandy. Take your time.*

I slide my phone back into my purse. "I should go." I down my martini, which might be a bad idea after the shots.

"Why? Sandy dropping off Jolie right now?" He sips his drink, his big body not moving.

"No, it's just…"

He sets down his drink. "What?"

I'm not sure if it's the lounge vibes or the alcohol clouding my thinking, but he looks good. Too good. "We work together and need to keep things professional."

He chuckles. "Do you think I'm trying to seduce you?"

"I think it would be ironic if I was the one you slept with after your long drought, and alcohol and celibacy don't mix well."

He chuckles louder, and his head falls back.

Holy shit, I want to slap myself to get it together. *You do not want Jax.*

Only the thrumming between my thighs tells me differently.

"Don't worry, I don't pursue where I'm clearly not wanted." He raises his hand and signals for what I hope is another round of drinks and not shots.

"Okay." I relax. This must just be a me thing then.

"How did you and douche meet?"

"At a club. Which should have been my first sign."

"And Jolie?"

"She was the best mistake I've ever made."

He smiles and it's genuine. The way he cares for my daughter makes me smile back.

"How long have you guys been apart?" Jax asks.

The waitress drops off another round of drinks, and I lower my head so Jax can't see my face. I'm most ashamed of how long I stayed, risking my daughter.

"Hey." He slides over to my side of the booth and puts his

arm around me. "What did I say?" His voice is full of concern, and for some reason, that makes me feel worse.

I shake my head, wishing he'd be mean to me right now. "Nothing." I slyly wipe my tears.

"Bullshit, I said something."

I continue shaking my head. "Nope. I'm good, but I really should go." I dig in my purse and drop a twenty on the table.

As I go to slide out, I realize he's blocking me and not moving. I look at him—Jax really is a gorgeous man. "I should've left him a lot sooner. That's all. Now can I go?"

My hip hits his thigh because he still doesn't move. "I'm sorry. I didn't mean to pry."

"Sure, you did. I think you get a kick out of seeing me upset."

His shoulders sink and he looks as if I popped his birthday balloon. "No, I don't. I think you're strong as fuck. I can't imagine raising a kid on my own. Hell, she sure wouldn't be as awesome as Jolie. We have our differences, but I figured that's how we got along. We take jabs at each other *because* we like each other."

"Like immature ten-year-olds who think the opposite sex has cooties?"

His arm drops and the warmth of his palm soaks into my skin through my shirt. His fingers rub my arm and I slowly move my gaze up to his. "I don't think you have cooties."

"Me either," I say, my eyes fixed to his.

"Frankie," he says, his voice low and sultry as he leans in.

"Yeah?" I hold my breath and wait for him to respond.

"I'm gonna kiss you now," he says right before his lips press to mine.

My eyes close—holy shit, the man can kiss. It shouldn't surprise me, but between my own sex drought and the fact that Michael was usually more drunk or high than sober, I can't remember the last time I was kissed like this. Like he's starved for me. Like he can't get enough. I love the way he lightly nibbles on my bottom lip right before he sucks it. Then without warning, he slides his tongue inside my mouth, tangling with mine.

A low groan rumbles up his throat and I grab his T-shirt, fisting it so he doesn't think he's getting away. His body pushes me against the wall at the end of the booth, his large hand holding my hips from bucking because I need something to grind against. Then his mouth is off mine and I whimper at the loss.

"Let's get out of here." His voice is gravelly and oh so sexy.

"But—"

He tosses money onto the table and hands back my twenty. "Do you not want to?"

"It's a bad decision," I say, leaning into him and hoping he'll put his lips on mine again.

"Yeah, it is, but because of your bet, I don't have much self-control right now. But if you don't want to, say the word."

This is a bad decision with consequences I don't want to think about because all I want in this moment is some pleasure. It's been so long since anything in my life was simply about me feeling good.

I press my fingers to my tingling lips. Fuck it. I'm taking it this time. "My apartment. They're not due back for hours."

"You underestimate my abilities," he says, taking my hand and dragging me from the Velvet Bar.

We barely reach my apartment door without touching or kissing in the elevator, down my hall, while waiting for me to get the key in the lock. Once the door shuts, I put on the latch in case Jolie and Sandy arrive home early for some reason. He kicks off his boots and picks me up by my hips, so I straddle him, attaching his lips to mine.

"I knew you'd be so fucking good," he murmurs into my neck before sucking my earlobe into his mouth.

After walking us back to my bedroom, he drops me and strips off his T-shirt, reaching behind his back with one hand and pulling it over his head.

I scramble to get out of my clothes. He's already stripped to his boxer briefs and crawled across the bed to me, hooking his fingers into my yoga pants and dragging them down my legs.

"I thought you weren't a bed type of guy?" I ask.

"Oh, you'll barely know we're on a bed when I'm done." He winks.

Then I'm naked in front of him and he hovers over me, his gaze heated and smoldering. There's something about a guy like him looking at you as though you're a goddess. I've never felt sexier, so I crawl on my knees to him. I touch the large bulge in his underwear, wrapping my fingers around his cock and sliding my fist up and down.

He bucks and his hand slides into my hair. I lower his boxer briefs and lick up his length before he backs up and pushes his boxers completely off. "I'll never last and I'm pretty sure we both need to fuck."

He's so right. He's always so damn right.

I lie down on my back as he grabs his pants on the floor and digs into his wallet for a condom. "How long has that been in there?"

He chuckles. "Don't worry, it's not expired." Then his voice lowers an octave. "On your stomach, baby."

I flip over, raising my ass in the air. His hands slowly run over the globes of my ass before he slaps it. I scream out, but damn, it felt good. It's as if he can read exactly what my body needs. When he dips his finger through my folds, I rub my pebbled nipples against the comforter, needing the friction.

"I guess I ruined your clean pair of panties after all?"

"You cocky mother—" I lose all thought when he presses his tip inside me and thrusts. "Oh shit."

His hand lands on my shoulder, pulling me back to him as he grinds into me. I've never been so turned on. I grow wetter the more sounds he makes behind me and the harder he slaps my ass with his free hand.

And when he leans over me and pinches my nipples with his fingers, it's almost game over for me. But Jax is just getting started.

CHAPTER FIVE

Jax

*T*his is a bad fucking idea. What was I thinking? Because now that my dick is inside Frankie, I'm not sure it will ever want to be anywhere else. She clenches around me and I circle my hips, then clench my ass, sliding in and out of her.

She moans and cries out and says my name as though I'm a god. Her ass is already pink and damn, what a beautiful sight it is.

Her head falls forward on the mattress. I take her hips in my hands, pulling her back as I thrust forward. I can tell she's right there. She deserves to have an orgasm that rocks her world, so there's no way I'm coming first.

I lie down over her back, my hands cupping her tits, my thumbs running over her nipples. Her back arches and I kiss her shoulder, pushing inside her. She's so wet and warm, I could stay here forever and be a happy man.

"Jax," she sighs and her head tips back to my shoulder. My lips are all over her face until I manage to take her lips in a fleeting kiss because it restricts too much movement. "I'm right there."

"I know you are." I slide my hand down from her tits, past her navel to her clit, then I slowly circle the nub.

"Oh God," she pants and her back arches again. "Don't stop."

"Don't plan to," I say, applying more pressure.

Her hand reaches down and locks around my wrist so I can't move. "Holy... seriously..."

Her entire body stiffens and a long, satisfying moan slips past her lips. A moan I want to hear with my cock in her mouth. Just the thought makes me harder inside her.

"Hold on, baby, because it's about to get rough."

I sit back on my knees, grab her hips, and push and pull her onto my cock until I'm the one stilling and pumping into her as my orgasm overwhelms me to the point that I see stars. We both collapse on the bed, a sweaty mess.

"Damn." I roll off the bed and open the closet before finding the bathroom that attaches to her room and the hallway.

When I return, she's still sprawled on the bed. I walk slowly as if I'm tired when I'm really committing her body to memory because I'm fairly sure this was a reckless, emotional, one-time thing between us. But hell, if she'd be up for a friends with benefits situation, I wouldn't object. She's an amazing lay.

I study the tattoos covering her back, all perfectly placed so everything melds together seamlessly. In my experience, women think about their tattoos a lot more than guys. Guys can decide in a night while women dissect what they want and where they want it, sometimes for what seems like a lifetime.

I pick up my boxers and I'm stepping into them when she turns to face me, her hands tucked under her head. Her confidence in her body is so damn sexy. I hate when someone gets shy after I have sex with them, wanting lights off or hiding under the blankets. But the woman in front of me is comfortable and confident in her body. That's why I'd love to ask Frankie the one question I never will—how she ever allowed her ex to treat her the way he did.

"Leaving?" she asks.

"Looking for round two? I know, I should come with a warning label." I wink.

Her eyebrows raise. "Man, you do think highly of yourself." She turns away and rolls off the bed, grabs a robe from the chair, and wraps herself in silk.

"You know I'm joking most of the time." She does, right?

She shrugs as though she couldn't care either way. "Where do we go from here?"

As she asks the question, the door of the apartment slams open into the chain lock she put in place. Both of our eyes widen.

"Frankie? I hope you're in there," a woman's voice calls. *Sandy.*

Frankie rushes off the bed and screams out to the hallway, "Yep, sorry, I was just being careful. Hold on, I'm just getting out of the bath."

Then she's back in the room with me as I try to get dressed as fast as possible, but she's throwing my clothes at me which makes it harder. She jogs down the hall as Sandy tries to open the door again. Frankie shoves it shut.

"Frankie?" Sandy asks from the other side of the door.

"Hold on." She throws one of my shoes at me. I fumble, but I catch it.

"Where am I going to go?" I whisper-shout.

"Frankie, I heard someone else. Are you alone?" The door opens again and slams into the chain.

"That's just the television," Frankie yells back.

"Sweetie, just open the door, I'm getting concerned and Jolie doesn't feel well."

Once I'm finally dressed, I hold up my hands at Frankie since she's running this show. She runs to the balcony door and bites her lip. I look out the door and shake my head. She's insane. I'm not going down the fire escape.

She holds her hands together in a prayer pose. "Please? I can't give Jolie the wrong idea."

"Which would be?" I whisper.

"That you and I enjoy spending time together without her."

Talk about a knife to the heart. I just gave this woman a very satisfying orgasm and she's ashamed of me?

I shake my head and step out onto the small balcony. Just as I turn around, she clicks the door shut and slides the drapes shut.

Damn, do I feel used and unwanted.

"Frankie, are you sure you're alone?" I hear Sandy ask.

I lower the fire escape ladder and crawl down it before we get caught. Truth is, if I got caught, it would only be a matter of time before it traveled back to our group of friends and I'm not interested in getting lectured by Dylan any time soon.

I PUT on the T-shirt my roommate, Kamea, designed and printed for me. I fucking love it. It's the perfect icebreaker to piss off Frankie since we haven't seen each other since I scaled down her fire escape like Spiderman.

I walk out of my room sporting the black T-shirt with the lettering "Jax Inked Me and I Loved It."

My other roommate, Knox, turns to his girlfriend and raises his eyebrows in accusation since she designed it for me. Yeah, I live with a couple.

"Frankie is going to kick your ass," Knox says.

I laugh. "That's the point." I grab my jacket off the hook on the back of the door and slip it on before picking up the container with the rest of the T-shirts in it.

"Hold up," Knox says.

I stop at the door.

"Tell her to accept my gift. That I'm wooing her." He nods in Kamea's direction.

I place down the container of shirts and put my hand on her shoulder. "He's wooing you. Not trying to own you."

"I've never thought he wanted to own me," she says. "Saving is more like it."

"I'm not trying to save you. I'm your boyfriend, and I'm helping you. Think of it as an early Christmas gift." Knox wraps his arms around her waist and pulls her toward him. "You have to let me do nice things for you."

"Not buy products for my company." Her forehead hits his chest.

I really don't want to be part of this. This is the downside of living with a couple. "I'm out." I pick the box of T-shirts back up. "Gonna show Seth first."

I laugh while leaving the apartment. I walk down the hall and knock on Seth's door. Evan, his girlfriend, tells me to come in.

One look at my shirt and Seth jumps up from the couch. "Has she seen it yet?"

I shake my head and open the door of their apartment to leave, too eager to wait for Frankie to see it.

"Let's go then," Seth says, joining me.

The three of us walk out into the hall as Kamea and Knox are leaving for their date.

"I'm gonna record this because it's gonna go viral." Seth pulls out his phone.

We all climb onto the elevator, but when the doors open in the lobby, Knox's mom is waiting.

"Mom?" Knox asks.

"Hey, Mama Whelan. I got something for you." Since this woman practically raised me, I kiss her cheek before setting down my plastic container to give her one of the T-shirts.

She reads it and beams like I knew she would. "I'll be proud to wear this."

"Um. no." Knox snatches it and tosses it back into the container.

"That's not nice. I'm proud to wear something Kamea designed that advertises Jax." She grabs it again before I shut the container. "You look very beautiful," she says to Kamea.

"Thank you, Peggy. Knox is taking me on a date." Kamea slides her arm through his.

"Why are you here?" Knox asks his mom.

"I have a letter. Jolie's." She digs inside her purse and holds it up. "I'm sure Frankie would want to know what Jolie asked Santa for, and I forgot to pass it on at the shelter that night. When you were younger, you'd change your mind the day before and I'd end up chasing the item down any way I could, so you'd believe in Santa." She looks at Kamea. "Glad those days are over."

"Come with me. I'm showing off my shirts to Frankie," I say.

"Oh, that's nice."

Oh, not so nice, Mama Whelan.

"Yeah, Frankie's going to kick him in the balls," Seth adds, his phone poised and ready.

"Well, let's go see the show before we head out," Kamea says.

Knox looks annoyed, but he shrugs. "Great idea."

We walk into Ink Envy. I shouldn't be this excited, but I'll admit, I was worried what it would be like for Frankie and me now that we've seen each other naked. This will cast aside any weirdness.

Frankie is behind the counter, her phone out in front of her. She glances up briefly and her cheeks turn pink when she makes eye contact with me.

Oh, don't you worry, I have the perfect distraction for us, Spark Plug.

Dylan's in the back, presumably tattooing someone, and Rian is up front with Blanca and Ethan. Sierra went to Sandsal with Adrian for some family function, so they aren't here.

I don't waste any time, opening the container, grabbing a shirt, and swinging it around my finger. "Who wants one?"

Frankie rolls her eyes. "I don't want anything from you."

"Oh, come on. Sit in my chair and you get one of these for free." I point at my T-shirt.

Seth is giddy with anticipation, his phone recording the whole thing. Knox groans and shakes his head. Typical cop reaction.

Frankie's eyes narrow as she reads. "Fucking hell, I'm quitting if you hand out those damn things."

Surprisingly, she doesn't say much else. Huh.

"Frankie." Knox's mom heads over to her, interrupting my big moment. "Jolie left this letter for Santa with me that day at the shelter." She hands her Jolie's letter.

Seth lowers the phone, just as let down as I am that my T-shirt didn't earn a better reaction from Frankie.

"Thanks so much. She told me she wrote Santa and gave it to Knox's mommy because she knows Santa. She won't tell me what she wrote and refused to write another letter because she said that he already knows what she wants."

Everyone laughs. That little girl is brilliant.

Frankie opens the envelope and pulls out the letter with a drawing. She reads it silently then narrows her eyes and reads it again. "You have to be shitting me?" She drops it on the table and her face loses some of its color.

"What? Something expensive? I'll get it for her," I say, picking up the letter. I read the letter and drop it as if I'm going to catch something from it.

My gaze falls to Frankie, and she cocks her jaw and nods.

"What's so bad?" Mama Whelan picks it up and reads it. "Ah, so cute."

Everyone steps forward.

Mama Whelan takes it upon herself to read it to everyone. "'I want Jax to be my daddy, and if he can't be my daddy, I want a puppy.'"

My stomach bottoms out. I walk away, silently tucking my container under my station. Holy shit, I thought the little girl was brilliant, but to want me as a dad means she's delusional.

41

CHAPTER SIX

Frankie

*L*ong after our friends have left Ink Envy, it's just Lyle, Dylan, Jax, and me. I'm trying to act cool. As though I don't care that my little girl is asking Santa for something I can't possibly give her. Even a puppy is off the market because my apartment doesn't allow dogs.

Thankfully, my next appointment is a long-term client who might help me decipher what to do—or she would if Jax wasn't twelve steps away. It's awkward enough that we slept together. Now he probably thinks I bribed Jolie to write that letter.

"Don't forget your shirt. Everyone gets one until I run out." Jax throws his latest client one of the black shirts he showed off earlier.

The shirts are a clever idea, but he knew they would piss me off. Why? I had no idea until the other night. Ever since

Jax arrived in Cliffton Heights and decided to retire from his traveling showcase tour, I've been up a lot of nights, trying to figure out why I loathe him so much.

Who cares if he sleeps with a lot of women? Then again, I haven't actually seen him with a ton of women. It's just that every woman who comes in here flirts with him, and it's like he's on autopilot, flirting back. Even if he slept with every woman in Cliffton Heights, what does that have to do with me? He's single. He's entitled to do what he wants.

But when he had me bent forward, ass in the air and his dick inside me, giving me the best orgasm of my life, I finally realized that he's my kryptonite. He's my chocolate cake and ice cream. He's my cigarettes, my vodka, and my crack. He's my vice. My body buzzes when he gets too near. Now I'm left with the aftershock of reliving the twenty minutes we fucked over and over again as I pleasure myself.

Which means if I have to move in order to get a puppy for Jolie, I will. Jax won't be stepping into the spot of my daughter's faux daddy.

"I'm heading next door to see Rian. Be back." Dylan throws on his leather jacket and walks out of Ink Envy, leaving us with a rush of cold air.

Now if only Jax and Lyle would leave so I can concentrate on the piece for my client who's about to show up any minute. I finalize some elements to get the stencil made.

Jax pulls out his journal, leaning back in his chair and sketching who knows what. Another design he can put on Instagram maybe. Although in the last two months, he hasn't posted nearly as much as he used to. I'd love to ask him why he returned here when he had this huge following on the road. It's something I would've loved to do if I didn't have Jolie, but she makes staying in Cliffton Heights worth it.

The door chimes and I've never been more grateful to see

my client, Hennessy. I stand and my chair rolls back. Jax glances toward the front of the shop.

"Hey, girl," Hennessy says and walks right by Lyle to the half wall, letting herself into the back area.

"Excuse me…" Lyle stops when she holds up her hand at him.

"She's good," I say. I wrap my arms around Hennessy, holding her tight.

"Whoa, okay. Is there something wrong?" She's too loud for her own good, so I pull back, slightly embarrassed.

"No." I shake my head, but I feel Jax's eyes on me.

"Don't have to stop the loving on behalf of us. Lyle and I can go get some oil for you two to roll around in," Jax says.

Hennessy circles around to face Jax. She hasn't come in since he started here—mostly because she's a wanderer and has been traveling around Europe for the past year. "Who are you? Dylan two point O?" She glances back at me and her eyebrows shoot up.

She likes what she sees. Who doesn't?

"If that means a hotter version of Dylan, then yes." Jax doesn't bother looking away from his sketchpad.

"Hennessy, this is Jax Owens. Jax—"

"Holy shit. I know you." She points at him, eyes wide. "You studied under Choi."

He finally looks at her. "I did."

"And you work here? With Frankie and Dylan?" I'm sure Hennessy doesn't mean to imply Ink Envy is beneath his talent, but her tone suggests otherwise. Funny, since she always comes to get her more holistic designs done by me.

"Dylan and Jax are childhood friends," I say.

"Oh, well, that explains it. Are you heading out on the road again soon?"

I'm trying not to take her interest personally, but her questions make me want to kick her out of my parlor.

"Nah, but I am doing a pop-up in Vegas next month," Jax says.

"You are?" I ask, forehead scrunched. He hasn't mentioned anything.

He leans farther back to look around Hennessy at me. "Yeah, wanna come? The only reason I didn't ask was Jolie."

"Yeah, true." I bite my lip. I can't very well ask Sandy to watch Jolie for the entire weekend. "Hennessy, are you ready?" I ask, changing the subject without answering Jax.

She turns slightly toward me, but most of her attention is still on Jax. "Um... yeah." She finally turns fully toward me.

I pick up the drawing I was working on. "You said on your ankle, right?"

"Oh, that's perfect. Exactly what I had in mind."

I begin to grab my stuff.

Hennessey adds, "But I think I'm going to change it to my inner wrist."

"Sure thing, just let me get the stencil done. I'll be back."

I head to the back room and hear Hennessy talking to Jax about his mentor, Choi. Then she goes on about how Jax really belongs in Los Angeles or, hell, New York City, asking what he's doing in Cliffton Heights. I never thought Hennessy looked down on me before, but I'm starting to think she does.

I'm about to exit the prep room when Jax's big body appears in the doorway.

"She talks too much." He steps inside.

I shouldn't care that he prefers to be in here with me rather than talk to Hennessy. She's gorgeous with her strawberry-blonde hair, bright green eyes, and cute figure that hasn't been through childbirth. Plus, she has one of those personalities that finds common ground with anyone.

"Sorry, but women are allowed to be seen *and* heard now." I move to slide past him, but Jax steps to the side to block me.

Hennessy is talking to Lyle, asking him a million questions.

"We need to talk," Jax says.

I flick my gaze up to meet his. Funny—he didn't seem in the mood to talk before. "About?"

"What happened the other day and Jolie's letter."

I place my hand on his chest. God damn, he's so firm. "Nah, we're good. And I'll handle Jolie."

"So we're cool?"

His question shouldn't throw me, but it does. I knew our drunken sex wasn't leading to anything—not like he was going to fall on his knees and want to date me—but his attitude stings. As for the letter… I'm Jolie's mother, I'm the one responsible for her.

"You're not going to tell her Santa isn't real, are you?" He slides onto the table, allowing his feet to hang off.

"No, and don't worry. It's really none of your concern." I move to leave the room.

"Hold up."

"What?" I turn around and he's staring at his hands in his lap. He has these long fingers and I've always admired the art they can create, but for some reason, my brain thinks now is a good time to imagine them inside me. I need help.

"I didn't mean for us to… you know. I mean, I just really felt like you needed a drink and someone to talk to. I hope you don't think I was trying to take advantage of you."

A hollow laugh falls out of me. "Relax, Jax, I don't expect anything from you. It was twenty minutes of my life."

He stares at me in disbelief, as though every time he sleeps with a woman, he has to file a restraining order. "Okay, fine. But with the Jolie thing… I can buy her a stuffed puppy or something."

I laugh again. "She'll be fine. Thanks though."

I walk out of the backroom before he suspects I'm lying.

That I can't stand the thought of the look on her face when she doesn't get either of her wishes.

I sit down on my stool beside Hennessy, who is sitting up and talking to Lyle about some bar in Sweden. "Ready?"

"Of course." She lies down and puts out her arm.

I had been excited about her coming in, eager to live through her experiences of traveling through Europe and picking up odd jobs here and there to get by. But now I'm just pissed off. At everything and everyone seemingly.

Jax walks out of the back room and sits at his station. His presence is as comfortable as if a bear were staring me down while I ate a big juicy burger.

"What's his deal?" Hennessey whispers. "Are you two…"

I glance over and he doesn't appear to be listening, so I shake my head.

"So he's fair game?"

My heart squeezes, but I nod, placing the stencil on her inner wrist.

"How are things with Michael then? And that sweet girl? Where is she?"

Just as she asks, Sandy walks in with Jolie, so I have to stop before I even start.

"There she is," I say, giving my daughter a big smile.

Hennessy coos about how adorable she is.

Jolie goes up to Lyle and shows him the ornament she made out of construction paper at school. He tells her how awesome it is.

"Hey, I wanna see." Jax tosses his journal to the side and rests his forearms on his thighs, waiting for her to walk by the barrier. The one she's really not supposed to go past.

"Sorry, Frankie, I got called into work. Someone called in sick." Sandy stands on the outside perimeter like clients are supposed to until they're called back.

"Bye-bye, Grandma." Jolie hugs Sandy's legs then opens the half door, heading over to Jax.

"Man, I'll be asking you to do my sketches for my tattoos soon." Jax picks Jolie up and puts her on his chair, looking over her ornament. "You going to put it on your tree?"

"When are we getting our tree, Mommy?" she yells across the room.

I hold one finger up to her and look at Sandy. "No problem. Go. Thank you so much."

"Sure thing. See you tomorrow, little thing." Sandy points at Jolie, and she giggles.

"I'll be the one with the pink backpack," Jolie says, and Sandy laughs.

Jax raises his hand for a high five, and Jolie smacks it as though he's the one who taught her that.

"Well, he's quite the little step-in daddy, huh?" Hennessy distracts me from seeing the way Jax's face lights up when he's around Jolie. "Cute. Never pegged him for the dad type, but now he's just a dad I'd like to—"

I start the needle and Hennessy's back falls back against the chair. Thank God she's silent now.

"I'm taking her over to Rian's. She's in need of a cookie fix," Jax says.

"I hope she has those monster cookies. They're my favorite." Jolie rubs her tummy and Jax picks her up as though I already said yes.

Sure, I could put my foot down and say no cookie for Jolie because I don't want her to get any more attached to Jax than she is. But the only other option is to let her sit here until I'm finished. So I nod and watch the two of them walk out of the parlor.

I pause to give either Hennessy or myself a breather—I'm not sure which.

Her head shifts from the door and back to me. "Okay, spill."

And even with Lyle there, I quietly tell Hennessy everything from my hatred for the man to how good of an orgasm he gives to my daughter wanting him to be her daddy. Damn, it feels good to let it all out.

CHAPTER SEVEN

Jax

$\mathcal{A}$s I walk Jolie over to Sweet Infusion next door, I have no idea how to navigate this new terrain I put myself on. Which I did. I can't blame anyone but myself for why this little girl asked Santa for the unthinkable.

When I first started at Ink Envy, I was annoyed but not surprised that Dylan would allow one of his renters to have her daughter all over the place. Sure, they'd tell Jolie she had to stay out of the area where we work, but do bulls listen to the cowboys who ride them? That's what it's like telling a small child she can't go somewhere.

After I learned a little more about what Frankie was going through with her ex, I can't deny my heart split open. I'm a foster kid. I've seen bad shit, so I shouldn't have been as affected as I was. But Jolie colored me a picture and it was over—the little girl won me over. But I'm the adult and I shouldn't have allowed it to go this far.

We walk into the bakeshop and no one is behind the counter. I know Dylan is here. Which means there's funny business going on in the back.

"Hey, we have a little person here," I say extra loud.

Rian comes out from the back, her face flushed pink and her apron askew. "Jolie!" She beams as though she's happy to stop her tonsil hockey with Dylan and spend some time with Jolie.

The entire shop looks like a Christmas store exploded in here. Rian does everything to the extreme, meaning there's more red and green in this store than Macy's in the city.

"It's so pretty." Jolie touches a piece of garland around the case of cookies. "You have a tree?" She rushes over to the small tree that Rian decorated with cookie ornaments in the shapes of hats and mittens.

"Do you have your tree yet?" Rian asks, opening the case of cookies and pulling out the monster cookie that Jolie loves. She comes over to Jolie's side and hands it to her.

"Wow, you used red and green sprinkles?" Jolie says.

Rian nods.

Dylan finally emerges from the back, his cheeks as flushed as Rian's. I'm not gonna lie, I kind of admire what they got going on and I'm happy as shit my best friend found the one for him. It's something he's been searching for since we were kids. He always wanted a family, and he's clearly going to have exactly what he wanted. But then again, Dylan's always been the more mature one out of the two of us.

"Not yet. Mommy said maybe tomorrow. Grandma said she'd give us her fake one, but…" Jolie runs her thumb over Rian's fake branch. "Mommy and I always get real." She sits down at the table. Luckily, Rian is winding down for the night, so no one else is here. "But Daddy usually takes it up the stairs and sometimes they fight over if it's straight or not.

51

Mommy said she doesn't need Daddy this year, that we're strong women."

Rian taps Jolie's nose and sits down across from her. "Girl power. I love it."

"Who brought your tree in for you?" Jolie asks.

Rian glances over her shoulder at Dylan and her smile slips. "You know what, Uncle Dylan would love to help your mom with the tree."

"Really?" Jolie looks at Dylan.

He side-glances me. Knowing Dylan, he wants to talk to me about that Santa list.

"Definitely. Even Santa needs his elves, right?" Dylan says.

"Speaking of Santa. Guess what came in the mail today?" Rian stands and goes into the back, then returns with a marker and the magazine.

"What's that?" Jolie asks.

"This is the toy catalog. I bet you can find some things to ask Santa for in here."

Again, Dylan looks at me. If Jolie weren't right in front of us, I'd flip him off.

Jolie pushes it away. "I already wrote my letter to Santa." She bites into her cookie and crumbs fall onto the table.

"But I heard you can change your mind. Santa doesn't mind," Rian says.

I'll give it to her, she's really taken it upon herself to fix the situation I created. She'll be an excellent mom someday.

"Nope, I don't want to change my mind." Jolie opens the catalog but doesn't pick up the marker.

"Well, you take that with you just in case." Rian stands from the table and glares at me. "Can I speak to you for a moment, Jax?"

"Nope," I say.

She stares blankly at me until I huff and follow her. It's easier this way anyway.

Once we're in the back, leaving Dylan to keep Jolie busy, Rian pulls out a big lump of red batter from the fridge and starts pounding it on the table. There are cooling racks with an abundance of baked goods, from cupcakes to cookies to cakes, off to the side.

She pounds the red dough, not looking at me. "That was my attempt to fix this for you."

"You don't have to fix anything for me."

Rian stops and puts both hands on the table, glaring at me. "And what is going to happen on Christmas morning when that little girl wakes up?"

Pound. Pound.

"Frankie said she has it handled."

She stops again. If I said she was glaring before, I was wrong. Now she's planning my death behind those blue eyes. "She's going to handle it?"

"Yeah." I move to grab a cookie, but Rian smacks my hand. "So no cookie for me?"

"No cookie until you undo what you've done." She points at me.

"Which is what?" I have to play dumb here. I'm fully aware of the position I've put Frankie in. I'm not happy about it, but damned if I know how to fix it.

"You better get that girl to write another letter and beg Santa for something else."

"And how do I do that?"

Pound. Pound. "Not my problem. Yours."

I pick up a cookie while she's too busy beating the shit out of whatever that is, and I take a bite. "Where's the sweet girl I used to share an apartment with? Dylan's having a bad influence on you."

I walk toward the exit, but she calls out to me.

"Jax!" I circle around, and the death glare she was giving me isn't there anymore. "This is big. It's one of those moments that can change Jolie and her outlook on the world. This is bigger than I think you realize."

I hold up my hand. Is she kidding me? Does she know how many memories I have of the shitty things that happened to me? "I realize that. Remember, I didn't have a happy childhood. I'm well aware of the way things can stick with you."

And just as the pity look is about to come over her face, I walk out. I'm not interested in anyone's pity.

"You don't have to do this," Frankie whispers as we walk through the rows of pine trees.

"Hey, I'm living out a childhood fantasy. This is a first for me too."

She stops for a second and I continue walking, catching up to Jolie. I should just take a sledgehammer and hit myself over the head with it. Rian's words keep repeating in my head.

"What about this one?" Jolie touches a tree, and a bunch of its needles fall to the ground.

We're a week and a half out from Christmas, so the selection isn't superb, but one of these will do.

"Let's keep looking. Check that one out." I point at one on the other side of the aisle.

Frankie joins me as Jolie runs forward, following the direction of my finger. "I'm serious, Jax. This is a lot and I totally had this under control."

I look her up and down. "You were going to carry the tree up all those stairs?"

"Hello, there's an elevator." She rolls her eyes.

"Okay, but you and Jolie were going to carry it the five blocks to your apartment by yourselves?" I stuff my hands in my pockets. It's fucking freezing outside.

"I was going to tip the guy nicely and maybe he'd do me a favor." Frankie laughs.

What, is she crazy? Showing some random guy she doesn't know where she lives?

"That's a good idea to put yourself in harm's way."

"I wasn't going to let him in the apartment."

I shake my head. "Well, now you have me, and since I've already been in your apartment and inside you, I'm not a threat." Jesus. Why did I have to bring that up?

She steps forward, her gaze darting to Jolie. "Are you implying that since you already saw me naked, you don't care to see me that way again?"

She's kidding, right?

"I never said that. Hell, if you want to start a little friends with benefits thing, I'm game."

"We'd have to be friends first." She gives me a saccharine smile.

Frankie's mitten-covered hand touches a tree branch, and she leans in, breathing in the scent of pine. I think someone might enjoy Christmas more than she lets on.

"Why friends? Enemies with benefits sounds a million times hotter." I elbow her.

Even in the cold, her cheeks glow with pink. I would've thought a woman like Frankie would be comfortable talking about sex.

She shakes her head. "Well, there aren't going to be any benefits. We both know those arrangements end badly. And we're already in some weird, twisted scenario, what with my daughter wanting you under the tree with a bow. We don't need to add any more complications to this situation."

Jolie runs over and takes my hand and Frankie's. "I found it. It's perfect."

She pulls us until we're at the far corner of the lot. Frankie and I look at one another in disbelief.

"This one?" Frankie asks, bending down to look at her daughter. Frankie runs her hands along one of the branches and none of the needles fall off.

"It's pretty," Jolie says.

"In a fugly way," I say.

Frankie whips her head back at me.

"Fugly? What does that mean?" Jolie looks at Frankie.

Frankie stands and examines the tree. "It's another way of saying unique."

I'm not sure what's to examine. It'll sit cockeyed in the stand. Good luck getting an ornament to hang, let alone a star or angel on the top. I bend down and look through the branches. Sure enough, the stump is shaped like a banana.

"Okay." Frankie nods and hugs Jolie to her front. "This is our tree this year."

I look around at all the other trees. At least they have a straight stump, even if their needles are raining down like snow. "Really?"

Frankie nods. "Yep, I think it's a great tree."

Again, my eyes fall to the tree Jolie picked. I swear it even has a sad face, as if it's the world's grumpiest tree, ready to say bah humbug.

"Okkkaaayyy," I say and turn around to find the tree guy.

When I track him down, he's on his phone.

"Hey, I need to buy the tree at the corner of the lot," I say.

"The blue spruce?"

"The fugly crooked one with all its needles."

He nods, clearly knowing exactly the one I'm talking about. "How about twenty bucks?"

"Twenty? That's it?" I pull out my wallet.

"I was gonna take it to the chipper tonight anyway.

Everyone just makes fun of it. I was even feeling sorry for the thing."

I hand him the money, realizing we're at least giving the tree a Christmas. Jesus, what is wrong with me? Why am I talking about a tree as if it's a person?

"I'll package it up for you." He walks back the way I came.

I grab two candy canes from the bin and take them over to Frankie and Jolie.

After the guy trims the stump and puts the tree through the netting, he bends down to Jolie. "You do know that this is a very special tree."

She nods, sucking on her candy cane.

"He needs plenty of water and don't put him by the heater."

Jolie nods and pets the tree. "Can I name him?"

Frankie sighs, but Jolie is either used to it or doesn't hear.

The guy says, "Absolutely. I've been calling him Earl. He seems like an Earl to me. But just like when you adopt a dog, you can change his name to whatever you like."

Jolie's eyebrows scrunch up and she glances back at Frankie and me. "Why would I change his name if he already has one? Is Earl ready?"

I chuckle. Kids don't get any cuter than this little girl.

"Here you go. Bye, Earl, this little girl is going to take good care of you. Have a Merry Christmas."

I feel as though I should tip the guy because Jolie is absolutely over the damn moon right now.

"Thanks. Jax is going to take Earl." She points at me, and I step forward and take the small tree from the man.

"Don't forget, water and no heat," the man repeats.

Jolie gives him a thumbs-up. Then we all walk out of the pop-up tree farm as though we're a family and just adopted Earl, the Christmas Tree.

How the hell did I get here? I have to be in some movie. There's no other explanation.

CHAPTER EIGHT

Frankie

Today is practically my last chance to deter Jolie from expecting what she asked Santa for. D-day is in four days. Thankfully, Jax told Jolie he couldn't stay to decorate Earl. I know he's trying to help by spending time away from her, and I appreciate it, but I can't help but wonder if the damage is done. I've loved watching Jolie water the tree and talk to it as though it's her friend. I wish she could have a sibling, but that's years away and only if I could ever learn to trust a man again.

I sit on the couch, sipping my coffee, staring at Earl. I'm shocked he hasn't lost many needles. I feel a kinship with this tree. I'm a little bent but can weather a storm too.

"Where are we going?" Jolie slides up on the sofa and hands me her socks, putting her feet in my lap. I told her I had a surprise for her after she was dressed and had her teeth brushed.

I take the socks and put one on her little foot. She's grown so much. Where did my toddler who could barely form words go? "We're going to see Santa."

She gives me the look. I never thought a five-year-old could give me the "you're crazy" look, but she's mastered it.

"What?" I put on her other sock.

"That's not Santa. Plus Knox's mommy said that Santa is her friend, and she was going to give him my letter, so I don't have to go see one of his helpers."

We've been over this so many times. But I have to get her to ask Santa for anything else before Christmas morning.

My phone buzzes on the table, but I ignore it. "I thought we'd go to the big toy store in the city, then go see Santa."

She blows out a breath. "Okay."

I'm shocked she agreed. I set down my coffee and pick up my cell phone, seeing Michael's name on the screen right before my phone dings a bunch of times. "Go get your sweater and bring me your brush to do your hair before we leave."

She jumps off the couch. Lately, we haven't had time to spend together just us, so I was excited for today. Until Michael called.

I read his stream of messages filled with vulgar language. I'd better respond before he shows up at the door. Instead of getting in a text war with him, I call him to confront this head-on. It rings once before he picks up. I step onto the balcony-slash-fire escape, shivering when the cold air hits me.

"Michael," I say.

"What the hell, Frankie? Sole custody? You act like I've tried to take her away from you. Why are you doing this?"

"I'm doing this because she needs consistency in her life." I don't want to throw Sandy under the bus, but I so badly want to call him out about leaving.

"She has it. I barely come around."

"Exactly." I look behind me to see if Jolie's there, but she's not.

"I cannot believe you're going to try to take her away from me. You know I don't have any money to fight you. My mom won't even give me any to fight you. Jolie's mine."

There was a time when I felt bad for Michael. I know his family history, that the addiction and physical assaults trickled down from his father to him. I think that's why Sandy harbors so much guilt. She stayed with Michael's dad until he died. The night I realized I had to leave Michael for good was when she told me that when Michael's dad took his final breath, she exhaled a sigh of relief. It was the first time since they'd been married that she felt safe.

I refused to be there in twenty years or allow Jolie to fall into the same pattern.

"Get clean and we'll talk."

"I am clean."

"Michael," I sigh.

"Mommy!" Jolie runs into the room.

I glance over my shoulder and she stops on a dime, staring at me outside. Her smile turns into a frown. She knows I come out here so she can't hear me.

I cover the receiver and poke my head in. "Why don't you water Earl really quick?"

"Earl? You're with some guy named Earl? And what the hell does that mean, water him?"

"Jesus, Michael, get off that shit."

"Listen, just give me some time. I swear I'll straighten out."

I'm used to this song and dance though, and I've fallen for it more than once. "As soon as you get clean, you can challenge the ruling. If things are good, you'll be granted visitation."

For Jolie's sake, I hope Michael gets clean one day, but he's not even close to hitting rock bottom. As much as I wish losing any custody rights to Jolie would be the bottom for him, it's probably not. Which tells me I'm making the right choice.

"How did they even find me anyway?"

"I know your hang-outs, and this is important. You can't keep floating in and out of her life, Michael. It's not fair to her, and it's not fair to me to have to pick up the pieces every time you say you're coming, and you don't. Or when you stop by and she thinks it's to see her but really you're looking to steal something to pawn or to ask for money."

"Goddamn it, Frankie!" A loud pounding sound echoes through the phone, and I think a door, or a countertop is absorbing his anger this time.

"I'm not changing my mind. Sign the papers and make this easy. Otherwise we'll go to court. I'm pretty sure it'll be the same result when they see what you've done while you're using. I may not have reported you, but I took pictures, Michael." I poke my head in to see Jolie talking to Earl as she waters him with the watering can we bought. "I have to go. She's here and I'm not having this conversation in front of her."

"I'm coming over for Christmas," he says.

"You're not welcome."

"As of right now, she's mine. I have rights to her."

"She's not a piece of property, she's a person," I say, my heart rate picking up at the thought of him showing up on Christmas morning.

"You better be there, otherwise..."

"Otherwise what?"

"Just be there, Frankie. With Jolie. You two are my family."

"We aren't anymore."

Another sound of him hitting something.

"I'm hanging up. Merry Christmas, Michael. I do hope you get the help you need."

"No, you—"

I hang up the phone and put it on silent. Closing my eyes, I inhale a deep breath of cold air. I've let him in before, but not this time. This time, things need to change for good.

"Ready, Mommy?" Jolie appears at the doorway to the balcony and looks at the phone in my hand.

"Yep. Let's go." I go back into the apartment, knowing my train ride into the city will be spent ignoring a barrage of texts.

I STARE out the train window as the buildings get closer together until we're in the city. I'm not exactly in the mindset I hoped to spend the day with Jolie in, but such is our life. I wonder what it's like to not feel as if something is coming for you all the time.

Walking around the toy store, Jolie sets her eyes on the rack of dolls. She kneels on the floor and touches each and every box.

"Would you like a baby doll like that?" I ask.

She purses her lips. "I'd like a brother or a sister."

My stomach drops. "Well, you could practice on a doll." I hope she takes the bait.

"The doll can't talk." She stands and walks farther down the aisle.

"Neither can Earl," I murmur to myself.

She stops at a scooter but doesn't linger. When I was her age, I would've died to have any of these toys.

"Crafts? You could ask Santa for some crafts."

"Mommy." Her small shoulders fall. "I already told Santa what I want."

"Okay, well, I have to get you something too. What do you want from me?"

She walks ahead and watches a few kids playing at a train table. "I told Santa two things, and he's gonna get me one of them, so I don't really need anything else."

She continues perusing the store while I watch. I'm so telling her this story when she's old enough. And hope her own child puts her in the spot I'm in right now.

"How about one of those dogs that barks, and you take for a walk?"

She shakes her head.

I look at my phone to check the time. "It's almost our time for Santa. We better go."

"Okay."

I take her hand, and we walk out of the toy store and down the block to where Santa is. I check-in with our name. Who knew nowadays you have to make an appointment to see Santa Claus and then you still have to wait?

As we inch up in the line, Jolie points out Santa's workshop, the little elves, and the fake snow. It's magical and she seems to be eating it up. Thank goodness.

Soon it's our turn and the elf opens the barrier for Jolie to go sit on Santa's lap, which she does with no problem. The woman takes a picture—as do I, because I'm not spending fifty dollars for them to print a picture on their color printer.

"Now what do you want for Christmas?" Santa asks in a jolly voice.

Jolie smiles at him. "It's okay, I know you're not him."

The kids close in line gasp and look at their mothers and fathers. I lower my head in embarrassment.

"I gave my letter to one of Santa's friends. I'm sure he's got it," Jolie says.

Santa doesn't even blink. "Well, Santa checks in with me. So if you tell me what you asked for, I'll make sure he got your letter."

She shakes her head. "Nope. He knows. Have a Merry Christmas." She hops off his lap.

The elf looks at me like *WTF, lady?*

"So sorry," I mouth and take Jolie's hand. While shoving her back into her coat, we head in any direction that leads away from Santa. "Jolie, why wouldn't you just tell Santa what you want?"

"I told you I wasn't going to."

I blow out a breath. "Let's just go home."

I'm silent on the train ride home because I'm going to have to break my daughter's heart on Christmas morning. Hopefully, she'll understand that she's asking for too much. Then I remember she's only five.

We get off the train and walk back to our apartment, but the hair on the back of my neck raises when we turn onto our block. I look around, not seeing anything unusual. I'm sure that by now, Michael has gone and gotten high, so he didn't have to feel anything about me suing him for full custody. We walk closer to our building and almost stop in my tracks.

"Daddy?" Jolie drops my hand.

I look up, finding Michael outside of our apartment doors.

"There's my girl." He holds out his arms, but she doesn't run to him as she once would have.

We slowly approach. Michael snatches Jolie up in a hug, but she remains limp in his arms.

"Aren't you excited to see me?" he asks.

"You should have called, Michael."

He lowers Jolie to the ground, and I grab her hand.

"I called you this morning," he says in a biting voice.

He's obviously been using, so I insert my key into the door and usher Jolie inside the building.

"Seriously, Frankie, you're just going to go inside and not let me see her?"

"Maybe we can make arrangements for you to see her, but no surprise visits anymore." I go to slide into the apartment door, but he slams the glass door shut before I can make it.

"*Mommy!*" Jolie cries.

I smile and hold up my finger at her, trying to appear relaxed. Circling around, he cages me against the apartment building.

"She's right there, Michael," I whisper.

He looks through the glass as though he had a momentarily lapse of memory. "She doesn't even want to be with me."

"What do you expect? You're never around. You're in and out of her life like a turnstile." I grip the door handle. Jolie tries to push it open, and I slam it shut with my butt.

He shakes his head but doesn't move.

"Just go," I beg.

His eyes stay on me and my hand cramps from holding the door handle so hard, but I'd never let go and let Jolie get in the middle of this. A car pulls up along the curb and squawks its siren.

"That your cop friend?" Michael glances over his shoulder and shakes his head. "This isn't over."

He walks away, but it isn't until Knox gets out of the car that I release my grip on the door. Jolie opens the door and runs over to him. He gives me an apologetic smile and keeps her occupied for a minute while I sit on the curb and pull out my phone.

Me: *Do you mind some guests for Christmas this year?*

Three dots appear immediately. And I know they'll both be super sweet about it.

Dylan: *I was kind of sick of Rian anyway. ;)*

Rian: *I need some girl time.*

Me: *Thanks. I promise we'll be gone right after Christmas.*

Rian: *Stay as long as you want.*

Dylan: *Need any help?*

I look at Jolie, who has come up beside me and cuddled in, looking as if she could fall asleep any second.

Me: *I'm good. See you tonight.*

Rian: *You have the key, let yourself in.*

If I had a minute to decompress, I'd probably burst into tears over having such good people in my life. But I don't have time to feel sorry for myself. I have to get my daughter somewhere safe.

CHAPTER NINE

Jax

Seth examines the tree, his head tipping right then left. "You paid money for this?"

"Earl. His name is Earl." Jolie's busy watering the tree. "What's your tree's name, Rian?"

"Yeah, Rian, what's your tree's name?" Seth mocks. One day Jolie might stomp on his foot when she figures out what sarcasm is.

"Um." Rian glances at their perfectly decorated tree with an "Our First Christmas" ornament prominently displayed. "Glenda?"

"Glenda?" I scoff.

Rian gives me that death stare like she did in the back of the bakery. "She's the good witch."

None of us say anything.

"Seriously? No one? Wizard of Oz…" Rian adds.

"The hottie in the big pink puffball of a dress?" Seth asks. He's walking on thin ice.

"As opposed to the one dressed in black with the green face. Yes, Seth. That one." Rian rolls her eyes.

Jolie walks back over. "Earl, this is Glenda. Remember we're her guests."

Seth raises his eyebrows at me.

I shrug, a little protective, like it's no big deal that Jolie's formed a relationship with a Christmas tree.

"So since tomorrow is Christmas morning, how long is Earl staying with us?" Seth asks.

After Frankie called Dylan about staying with them for a few days, I got the lowdown from Knox that her ex had cornered her at the apartment. Although I want to find her ex and ask him why he'd think that's appropriate to do in front of his little girl, I refrain because it's really none of my business. Besides, I don't want to make things worse for Frankie.

But Jolie demanded that Earl had to come too. Frankie only lives seven blocks away, but Dylan and I had to carry Earl here, fully decorated, while Jolie acted like an overprotective mother watching her son get a tattoo.

"As long as he's healthy," I say.

"Jolie waters him every day," Rian calls from the kitchen. "Glenda's losing needles like she's aged ten years, but Earl there is still fully covered."

Seth crosses his arms, inspecting the difference. "Way to hold up, man. Stayin' healthy for the ladies."

I raise my eyebrows at Seth because he's talking to the tree.

"Want to help me, Jolie?" Rian asks from the kitchen, cookie cutters in the air.

It's Dylan's late night at the shop and Frankie was booked solid. Since I'm pretty much appointment only through the holidays, I came over here on a last-minute quest to change Jolie's mind about what she's expecting tomorrow morning when she wakes up.

"So did you get it yet?" Seth whispers.

I grab my beer and walk out to the balcony that overlooks Ink Envy and the street below. I've yet to talk to anyone about the Santa letter and since tomorrow's D-day, I guess I'm going to Seth for advice. He's a pretty cool guy. I haven't known him as long as Knox and Dylan, but I think I can trust his judgment. He follows and we rest our forearms on the cold metal railing.

I ask, "Get what?"

"The dog of course. Why? Are you thinking a wedding ring?"

"What?" I screech.

"Your answer was vague." He sips his beer.

"I'm not getting either. Frankie said she'd handle it, but from what I hear, Jolie's still adamant about the whole 'I wrote Santa a note' thing. Rian tried to give her a toy catalog she wanted no part of. Frankie took her toy shopping. She's going to bed expecting me with a bow on my head and a pin with Daddy written on it in the morning. Either that or a four-legged furball that she can't have in her apartment."

As though Winston, Rian and Dylan's dog, knows what we're talking about, he waddles out with us and lifts his leg on the fake grass pad they have out here for him. The life of a dog in a city. All Frankie's got is a fire escape she thinks can be used as a balcony. I rub my calf. It still hurts from the fall that day.

"You guys are screwed. Did I ever tell you the story about how my brother ruined it all for me? By the time I was five, I no longer believed. It sucked because it's like parents get lazy once they find out you know. There are no more surprises.

They might as well just wrap the gifts up right in front of you. I'm still pissed about it. Being the youngest sucks."

I finish my beer and allow it to dangle from my hand. "Shit, you don't even want to know what it was like for me."

Although Seth would listen to my pitiful ass story, I'm not going to tell him how I don't even remember ever believing in Santa Claus. Which is what happens when you end up at a foster care house where Christmas morning is like every other day. The only gift you get is one that someone donated from a card you filled out with your name, age, gender, and two items you might want. Some years you got something and some you didn't. The older you got, the less chance you had of receiving anything.

Thinking about my depressing childhood, I realize there's no way I can let Jolie wake up tomorrow morning and not get what she wants. I turn away from the street and look inside at her laughing with Rian as they cut cookies and lay them on the baking sheets. I can't be the reason her belief in the magic of Christmas is stripped away.

"I'll be back. I gotta go," I say.

Seth laughs. "Not without me, you aren't."

———

GOOD THING I never gave my key back to Rian and Dylan after I moved out. Not that it matters much. If one of them is home, the door is usually unlocked. As with most of us who live on this floor. Knox swears one day someone is going to rob us all blind. And he's probably not wrong.

I slip off my boots outside the door and tiptoe into their apartment. Glenda and Earl are still lit up while sunrise is filtering in through the windows. Presents fill the area under the trees already—probably most of them for Rian from

Dylan. The guy goes overboard. Then again, here I am delivering a puppy.

I place the box under the tree, thankful Winston must be in the bedroom with Dylan and Rian. Dylan might kick my ass if my puppy hurts their precious little dog.

I'm tiptoeing out when the bathroom door opens. I freeze as if whoever it is can't see an over-six-foot man standing in the room.

Rian yelps. Her flannel red, white, and green plaid pajama pants and shirt that says "Let's get Merry and Jolly" shows how much she loves this holiday. Who has specific pajamas for a holiday?

"What are you doing?" she whispers, walking across the room.

"Just delivering my present."

The pup whines in the box.

Her eyes widen and shift to the box and back to me. "You didn't."

"You told me to fix it. This is fixing it," I whisper and point at the box.

The puppy whines again, so Rian walks over, opens the box, and peeks in. She falls to her knees and picks up the small brown dog. "Oh, he's a cutie." She lets the dog lick her face and I wince thinking about Dylan kissing her after. "But Frankie is going to kick your ass."

"She's not going to know I did it." I give Rian a meaningful look and backtrack toward the door.

She puts the puppy back in and closes the box. "She's going to know. I'm not taking responsibility for this."

I raise my hands. "I couldn't let Jolie wake up and realize what a hoax Santa is."

"And when she asks why you're not her daddy?" Rian asks.

"Santa attached a note."

She peers down at the box where I secured the note I wrote while pretending to be Santa.

"Jax," she sighs.

"This is me handling it."

What does she want from me? Should I apologize nonstop because Jolie is attached to me? Never did I think she could see me as her dad. I'm not meant to be a dad. Growing up, I had no example of what a dad even is.

"Just don't let it suffocate." I walk out the door, grab my boots, and disappear into my own apartment.

I wish I could be there when Jolie wakes and discovers her present. I can only imagine how excited she'll be when she pops off the lid.

I slide back into bed, wishing sleep would come, but it doesn't. I hear Knox and Kamea having morning sex in his room next to mine, so I throw off the covers and decide to take a shower. Letting the water warm up, I close the bathroom door—since I'm showering—and take a piss before stepping into the water. I'm mid-shampoo when a loud banging sounds on the apartment door. Since Knox and Kamea are probably mid-orgasm, I rinse, shut off the water, and step out, wrapping a towel around my waist.

I open the door and find Frankie's fist in the air. She stops and her gaze falls down my body.

"Are you here for your Christmas present?" I grin. I can't help but want to rile her up.

Her eyes narrow and she places her hand on my chest, pushing me into the apartment.

I hold up my hands. "Oh, I like this take-charge side of yours."

"How could you? I can't have a dog in my apartment!" Then she pulls the letter out of her back pocket. "And this?" She plasters it to my wet chest.

73

I debate denying it but figure what the hell. "I handled it. We couldn't just ignore it."

Hell, I put a lot of thought into that letter and I think it was a damn good way to make Jolie understand she can't ask Santa for a daddy.

"I was handling it," she says. "I'm her mother."

"Either it was me or a puppy under that tree. She had to get one."

She throws her arms in the air. Hell, she really is damn attractive when she's angry. Turns me on. If she were mine, I'd probably try to piss her off on purpose.

"Why? Why do you care about her so much?" Her angry tone dissipates, and she sounds more like she's exhausted from fighting me. Knox's door opens, and Frankie raises her hand. "Merry Christmas, guys."

"Merry Christmas. What happened?" Knox asks, walking out in his pajama pants and no shirt.

Frankie motions to me. "He got her a puppy."

Knox laughs but bites his lip. See? He doesn't see a problem.

"What's going on?" Kamea asks, stepping out of the bedroom.

Knox turns Kamea back toward the room and they shut the door.

I stand there in silence.

Frankie throws up her arms again. I love her "Bah Humbug" tank top with a pair of boxer shorts. Fits her perfectly and my mind wanders to wondering whether she's wearing any panties.

"Fine. Just stand there and not say anything. I'll deal with the aftermath. I'm used to it anyway." She charges toward the door.

I should let her go. Let her be angry at me. At least I made Jolie happy.

But for some reason, words fall out of my mouth. "Because I know what it's like to wake up and not get what you want. Because I once wished for a family. Because I was disappointed when I was her age, and I can't sit back and watch it happen to her. Because she's five and she should be happy and innocent and go on believing in Santa."

Frankie slowly turns around. She's lost all fight, which means I might as well have put on a pussy hat for the day. "Jax—"

I raise my hand. "Maybe I overstepped. This was just my way of fixing it."

She releases a deep breath and doesn't say anything until the silence is nice and thick in the room. "Congratulations, Daddy."

"What?" I croak. We used protection, there's no way...

"You're half owner of a new puppy named Gumdrop."

Relief washes through me, but then the panic returns. "You're kidding, right?"

She smirks and shakes her head. "Nope." Her hand lands on the doorknob, but she turns around. "Oh, and Gumdrop is using Dylan's boot as a chew toy. So fatherly duty calls." She shrugs and walks out the door.

Knox opens his door, laughing. "Who told you to get a puppy?"

"Seth thought it was a good idea," I say.

Knox laughs even harder. "Don't ever ask Seth's opinion on what to do."

My head rolls back. Fuck. What the hell did I get myself into?

CHAPTER TEN

Frankie

*T*hree days after Christmas, Jolie and I are back in our apartment—Sandy assured us that Michael has left for the west coast. Mr. Holder told me that with Michael not here to fight my motion, the path to getting full custody might be smoother, but I'm not naïve—Michael will be back.

"Come on, Gumdrop." Jolie yanks at the leash. Poor dog.

"Remember we have to teach him to walk on a leash."

Trying to keep a dog hidden in my apartment hasn't been as hard as one would think. Luckily, Gumdrop is pretty quiet, and we're using puppy pads as a potty training technique.

"He really wants to see Earl."

"Well, Earl is with Glenda at Rian and Dylan's, remember?"

Jolie sits down and pouts. "Why didn't we stay there?"

She would love nothing more than to live in the Rooftop Apartments with everyone, but it's not possible. She's not old enough to realize that.

I ruffle her hair as I walk by, packing my bag. "Because that's not our place."

"What happened to my letter from Santa?"

"Hmm?" I play dumb because last I saw it, the letter was suctioned to Jax's naked chest dripping with water. He might as well have been naked because it was all I could do not to tackle him and give myself a Christmas gift that morning. He played my body perfectly the first time we were together, and I can't imagine once he's attuned to all my likes and dislikes how much more mind-blowing it would be.

"The letter that said he can't give me a daddy."

First, I sleep with Jax and find out what a fantastic lover he is, then he goes and writes the sweetest letter to my daughter, pretending to be Santa. I'm pretty sure Jax doesn't even understand the catch he's coming off to be. At least in my eyes.

The letter said that she's a girl anyone would want to be a daddy to, but he can't make that wish come true. But he hopes that she enjoys the puppy.

"I don't know, but we gotta get going. I have an appointment in a half-hour."

Unfortunately, school is out, which means Jolie spends her time with me at the shop until Sandy gets off work. Even then, I can't expect Sandy to be at my beck and call all the time.

"Can I at least go over and see Earl during lunch?" She slides off the couch and I help her with her boots.

The fresh snow isn't Gumdrop's friend, so I scoop him up and put him in my oversized purse with his leash and collar. "As long as Dylan says it's okay."

"He will."

What must it be like to have all these adults wrapped around your little finger? Stopping at the mailbox, I remember I forgot to get my mail last night, so I use my key to open the compartment, then shove it all in my purse to look through during my break today.

Jolie and I walk out of the apartment and the snow flurries whirl around us. I put a few coins in the meters as we pass by. Just a small good deed I can do for others this time of year.

"Can I do it, Mommy?"

I hand her two quarters. "Sure."

She puts them in, and I tell her great job. We walk the seven blocks until we reach Ink Envy, but I can't go in right away because we have to walk Gumdrop around until he goes to the bathroom. I shiver while Jolie walks back and forth, tugging on his leash because the dog doesn't yet grasp the concept.

"Come on, Gumdrop," I say in a nice tone to spur him to go to the bathroom. I bend down and nudge his butt to get him moving, but you'd think he's got brakes on those four legs. "You gotta walk."

Jolie huffs, and my head falls back in frustration. I need to get in the shop and get started. Then I look inside Ink Envy and there's Jax, sipping his coffee while coming back from the breakroom. I swoop up Gumdrop and grab Jolie's hand, tugging her along.

I swing the shop doors open and shove Gumdrop in Jax's arms. "You're on duty."

He fumbles to catch the dog and keep a hold of his drink, losing the battle. His coffee falls to the floor. "What?"

"Jolie, take off your coat and stomp your boots on the mat."

She sheds her coat, hangs it on the coat hook, and jumps

up and down on the rug. Then she sets her eyes on Jax and Gumdrop.

"He won't walk on his leash," she whispers. "Mommy's getting mad."

Jax hands Gumdrop to her. "Watch him until I get this cleaned up?" He sends a glare my way.

She sits in the waiting room with Gumdrop on her lap while Jax grabs paper towels from the back room to clean up.

"You could be nicer about it," he says to me softly so Jolie can't hear.

Lyle walking in keeps Jolie busy as he asks questions about Gumdrop.

"My mornings are busy enough without having to sneak a dog in and out of my apartment, teach it to walk on a leash, and oh yeah, clean up after it. Plus the thing is chewing the legs of my kitchen table. As though it wasn't already a piece of crap." My frustration gets the better of me and my voice raises a bit.

"Okay, I said I would help."

"That's kind of hard to do since you don't live with us."

"And what do you want me to do? Split custody? He's Jolie's and Jolie is yours."

I clench my fists and growl. "Jax, I swear."

I stomp away to Dylan's office for some much needed space. There's so much going on right now: Michael and trying to get sole custody, the constant worry about whether I'm doing the best thing for my daughter, the fact that I slept with Jax and he's able to act as though it never happened, and I have a puppy to care for. Since two of the biggest stressors in my life have Jax's name attached to them, I'm blaming him.

The office door opens and Jax walks in, holding up his hands. "I come in peace."

I roll my eyes. "This isn't funny. I had enough on my plate

before you bought her that puppy. It put me in a shitty position."

He nods and rests his ass on Dylan's desk, his hands on either side of his hips. "I'm sorry."

"Don't apologize because you think it's what I want to hear."

"I mean it. I do. I overstepped."

"Yes, you did. But I understand why you did." I blow out a long breath. After his declaration on Christmas morning about his childhood, I understood why he got Jolie the puppy, but I'm drowning right now. "It's fine. I just have to get through the puppy phase and find another place to live. Easy-peasy." I stand, unable to handle feeling sorry for myself anymore. "It's fine, I'll manage."

He grabs my wrist, pulling me back toward him, then rests his hands on my hips. "I truly am sorry."

We're millimeters apart and he's looking at me like he wants to kiss me. I hold my breath. I want him to, which I shouldn't.

As we lean in, I pull back. "You can't kiss it and make it all better." I wiggle out of his hold and bolt from the room.

Get a grip, Frankie. You've dealt with worse than this.

I'm GUESSING Jax has no more appointments today, but then I don't know why he's here either, because he spends majority of his day trying to train Gumdrop to walk on the leash. He and Jolie walk back and forth in front of the window.

"I've never seen Jax so determined," Dylan says from his chair. "Winston took to the leash right away, but in obedience school, another guy said his dog still runs away every time he shows his dog the collar."

I narrow my eyes at him. "That might be a piece of information you share after Gumdrop walks on his leash."

Dylan laughs. "He will. The instructor said that the dog must have had a bad experience with his leash before he got him from the shelter."

"Well, the way Jolie tugs on it, so will Gumdrop."

I swivel around in my chair. In between clients, I gave Jax hell, but truth is, I'm not sure what I would do without him or Dylan or all the rest of their friends. They help me with Jolie, and they help me sort my shit out with Michael.

"I was getting my mail last night and guess what I noticed?" Dylan says, putting on his gloves to put the stencil on his client.

"What?"

"The apartment downstairs opened up." He raises his eyebrows as though that's an option for me.

"I have an apartment."

"An apartment your ex knows the location of, one you can't have a puppy in, and if you want Jax to pay for getting you that puppy, maybe you two need to be closer so he can take care of it half the time."

I lean back in my chair. "I'm not sure it's a good idea that we live that close to each other."

"I know, he's so hot. I'd be prancing around in my bra and panties, hoping he popped in," Dylan's client says out of nowhere. She's one of his regulars and very open with her sexuality. Take right now, for example. Her ass is practically out for everyone to see as she gets her hip done. Dylan could've taken her to a private room, but she didn't want to.

"I mean more because the police might be called when I strangle him."

"Good thing a cop lives in the building," Dylan says with a chuckle.

"I'm just not sure it's the best place for us. But the puppy *is* driving me crazy, and I'd like nothing more than to make Jax pay."

"Jolie loves him though, and just so you know, Winston thinks Earl is his own pee tree, so I apologize in advance."

"Who is Earl?" Dylan's client asks.

While he tells her the story of our names for Christmas trees, I look out the window and see Jolie jumping and clapping. A minute later, Jax jogs by the window with Gumdrop prancing behind him before the dog stops dead in his tracks. But Jax takes it as a win as he swoops Jolie in his arms, swings her around, and they both bend down and pet Gumdrop, praising him for doing such a good job.

Seriously, how are my ovaries supposed to survive this? Jax with Jolie was enough to break the hatred I feel for the man, but add on a puppy and I'm supposed to pretend not to notice all his good qualities?

I want Dylan to think I don't want to move into their apartment building because I'm afraid I might kill Jax, but the opposite of that is what scares me so much. I could fall hard for him—only to find myself heartbroken and unable to care for my daughter. I could bring a father figure into her life who would be ripped away from her—again. Jolie has to come first, and if I'm ever going to choose a man to love, he can't be one with a reputation of running away from his problems.

But damn, Jolie hugs Jax, her arms tight around his neck, and the fact that it can't be him makes me a little sad. I hope he knows he'll make a great dad one day—whenever he grows up.

I grab my purse to distract myself from the view and decide to go through my mail before my next client arrives. I pick up what I think is the invitation to Blanca and Ethan's winter wonderland wedding, but it's dripping onto the floor. I pick up the rest, and sure enough, they're all soaked.

"*Ugh!*" I empty everything in my purse out on my bench and it's all soaked with pee. "I honestly cannot handle this."

The door opens and a rush of cold air comes in.

"Gumdrop walked, Mommy!"

"Yay, and no worries about his bladder, because he emptied it in my purse."

Jax laughs, which makes Jolie laugh. But all I can do is stare at the invitation to the wedding. All this and I have to find a date to a wedding. Lately my life has more problems than solutions.

CHAPTER ELEVEN

Jax

*T*he day after New Year's, I arrive at the veterinarian office to find Frankie already there and checking her phone with raised eyebrows.

"I'm not late," I say, walking right by her.

"We had to be here early to fill out paperwork."

"Which you could have done," I say, picking up Gumdrop. She's so hell-bent on us co-owning this dog, she can't fill out the paperwork herself?

"He's half yours," she says, following me inside.

The person behind the counter smiles and hands me a clipboard. I take it and sit on the bench, putting Gumdrop on the bench next to me. Frankie comes over and puts him on her lap.

"You know you're treating me like I'm a teenager, like you have to prove some point that I was irresponsible." I scribble my name on the sheet.

"Yes, because buying a dog for someone else *is* irresponsible." She crosses her legs and leans against the wall, cracking her neck. She looks exhausted.

"Jolie asked for one."

"Yes, and you need to learn that not everything Jolie asks for she gets."

"Why not?"

"I didn't see you jumping out of a big giant bag on Christmas morning, offering to be her daddy." She raises her eyebrows.

I feel like we're just going round and round in this conversation. I finish filling out the paperwork and hand it back to the woman.

"You'll split the amount, I'm told. Ms. Grant explained the situation." The receptionist is nice, but she's clearly taking Frankie's side.

After I sign the credit card slip, I fold up the receipt and stick it in my wallet, which I shove in my back pocket.

We sit and wait, neither one of us saying much. Finally, a lifetime later, our name is called, or at least Gumdrop's name is.

The tech is young and hot, and she definitely likes what she sees with me. Hey, call me an asshole if you want, but her eyes linger for longer than is appropriate. Even Frankie notices because she huffs.

"So Gumdrop is a new pup, huh? I just have to ask some questions." The tech is bubbly and talks baby talk to Gumdrop. Why do people do that? It makes my balls shrivel up. "Where did you get him?"

"I bought him from a pet store." You'd think it would be hard to get a dog on Christmas Eve, but it turns out I'm not the only one who bought a dog for Christmas. Hell, I almost had to pay double to get the thing.

"I would have adopted one," Frankie says, smiling.

"I was strapped for time." Part of me felt guilty buying a brand new shiny puppy instead of adopting a shelter dog, but I didn't have any options.

The tech smiles. "It's okay. All dogs need a home." She does the baby talk again.

Frankie makes the sound she does when she's annoyed but doesn't want anyone to know. She did it a lot when I first came on board at Ink Envy, but now she openly sighs or huffs or groans at me. It's our own form of communication.

"The doctor will come in and look him over. There are some shots she'll go over with you."

"Shots?" I ask with wide eyes.

Frankie chuckles.

"No worries, he's young, so as long as we make it a positive experience, he'll be fine." The nurse runs her hand over Gumdrop and he's ready to roll over on his back and coo from the looks of it. "I'll be right back." She gives Gumdrop a treat that he gobbles up.

Frankie and I stand in the small room in silence that I eventually decide to break. "I can't believe how much work a dog is."

Frankie looks over her shoulder as she pets Gumdrop, his front paws up on her. "Really? You never thought a four-legged animal that survives on food and water and attention might be a lot of work? It never crossed your mind?"

I point at her. "There you go again. I thought we were shoving all that animosity under the bridge and moving on?"

"Yeah, but seriously, you didn't think it through."

I shrug. "I never had a dog. I mean, one of the houses I lived in did, but they kept it outside all the time."

She sits down next to me, and Gumdrop climbs over the arms of the chair into my lap, then he curls up.

I pet him. "I know, I'm the calm one. She's high strung."

86

Frankie groans, and I look away before she sees me smiling. Why do I love pissing her off so much?

The veterinarian walks in and turns out she's just as hot as the tech. What kind of place is this?

The tech follows the doctor in, and Frankie's gaze sets on me as though I'm going to make a crass comment or something. Truth is, the baby talk is a complete turn-off. And even if it wasn't, my dick only responds to one woman in this room and it turns out she's the one who wants nothing to do with him. At least not more than once.

"I hear we got a new puppy?" Dr. Renee, as her lab coat states, says.

"One of us bought it and the other is taking care of it," Frankie says. I poke her with my finger, and she sighs. "I mean yes, we're raising the puppy together."

"Together?" Dr. Renee asks. "You live together?"

"No," Frankie says way too fast for me not to be offended. "He bought it for my daughter."

"Oh, that's so sweet," the tech coos with a high-pitched voice. "How old is she?"

"She's five," Frankie says.

Dr. Renee looks at Frankie, and they share some kind of look that makes me think they're having a silent conversation. And I'm pretty sure what they're saying is what kind of a dickhead buys a little girl a dog without asking the girl's mom?

"Are you two a couple?" Dr. Renee asks, then raises her hand. "I don't mean to pry, I'm just trying to figure out the together part. Puppies need consistency."

"Well, Gumdrop is at my house every night, but we work together, so I bring the puppy into work, then he's Jax's responsibility."

Dr. Renee chuckles then nods as if she's seen our case before. I'm certain she hasn't. If someone told me a year ago I was gonna be in a vet's office with a dog I bought Frankie's daughter, I would've asked what planet they're from.

"Okay, well, that could work, but I do suggest you go to obedience training. That way Gumdrop will learn to listen to you both, and the two of you will be on the same page."

"That would be a first," Frankie mutters.

The vet takes off her stethoscope and listens to Gumdrop's heart.

"And how much is obedience training?" I ask.

Frankie whips her head in my direction.

Dr. Renee holds up her free hand while she listens. After she's done, she puts the stethoscope around her neck. "Heart sounds really good." She turns to the tech. "Tori, why don't you go get the packet for new owners? Mr. Owens should probably know the ramifications of his purchase."

Frankie laughs and I stare blankly. I'm a straight-shooter, but I'm not rude either. Although I want to tell this woman off, I don't want to rearrange my schedule again to find a time where Frankie and I can go to another vet, so I let her comment go.

Dr. Renee surprises me when she continues. "I don't mean to offend. It's just a lot of people like the idea of a pet at Christmas, but they don't think it over. Then a lot of those dogs end up in shelters. Clearly, you two have an unusual set of circumstances and I do hope it works out, especially for your daughter. But I can admit to being skeptical."

"Are you throwing shade that we can't raise a dog?"

"Jax." Frankie gives me her favorite "shut the fuck up" look.

"I'm merely suggesting that it's hard, and if you're not even committed to being together yourselves—"

"We're just co-workers." Then I put up my hand. "You know what, you're our vet, not our conscience, so let's get this over with."

Dr. Renee leans back on the counter, and a tear slips from her eye. Frankie glances at me and nods as though she's telling me to take care of it.

I officially have no idea what the hell is going on.

Before I can say anything, Dr. Renee raises her hand. "I'm sorry. I'm acting ridiculous. My long-term boyfriend broke up with me on Christmas. I bought him a puppy, thinking we'd raise it together, and now I have the puppy and he's in Bermuda with his new girlfriend he met while buying me an engagement ring."

"What?" Frankie asks, and I look on with disbelief.

Dr. Renee nods and more tears flow. "We met in vet school, and he just said that you know when you know. And he thought it was time for us to get married, but then he met Stacy and he felt something he never did for me."

Frankie grabs a Kleenex and hands it to her. "Men are assholes."

Dr. Renee looks and nods at me. "Don't worry, he seems to know he's an asshole."

"I do. I might be an even bigger asshole than your ex. I bought a puppy for a kid who's not mine," I say, trying to lighten the mood. There's way too much estrogen in here.

They both laugh. Tori walks in and clearly figures out pretty quickly what's transpiring.

She shakes her head. "I'm going over to his house and leaving all the fecal samples we get there. It'll be a surprise for him when he comes home from Bermuda."

Then we're all laughing.

Dr. Renee blows her nose and washes her hands. "Okay, thank you for understanding. Let's administer the shots now."

Gumdrop's eyes widen along with my own.

"We'll be right back." Dr. Renee leaves.

I tug on Frankie's coat. "I'm not sure I can sit here for the shots."

"You're a tattoo artist," she says, looking at me as though I'm crazy.

"Shots and tattoos are different. The people coming to get a tattoo want one and the needle moves so fast you can barely see it," I shamefully admit.

"Jax, we are in this together. You will not make me do this by myself."

I swallow past the dryness of my throat. "You don't understand, I hate needles."

"No one likes them," she says.

I inhale, not wanting to seem pathetic. Fine, I'm sure I can do this. I just won't look. Gumdrop looks at me over Frankie's shoulder with those sweet brown eyes. Literal puppy dog eyes. *Sorry, buddy.*

Dr. Renee comes in and places three needles on the counter. "That's good, Frankie, hold him just like that."

"Oh no, Jax was going to hold him." She tries to hand him off, but Tori stops her.

"He's relaxed, let's keep him like that."

I'm blessed with Frankie's death stare again because she's stuck in this position. I could easily duck out, but I'm sure Frankie would drag me back by my boots.

After Dr. Renee is all gloved up and ready to administer the shot, Frankie looks over her shoulder.

"It's really quick," Dr. Renee says.

Gumdrop wiggles and I pet his head to calm him, stepping closer to Frankie and putting my arm around her waist. She winces when he squirms, and she has to grip him tighter. I turn away so I'm not looking, but I'm trying to be there for her.

Then Dr. Renee administers the needles. It isn't until the third that Gumdrop realizes what's happening, but then he's not having any of it. Frankie can't keep control of him any longer, so they try to do peanut butter off a spoon, a treat, but nothing is working. Finally, Tori has no choice but to be a little more forceful with Gumdrop and the shot gets done.

"Excuse me," I say, walking out of the room and into the bathroom where I lose my entire breakfast in the toilet.

Shit, I hate needles.

After rinsing my mouth and washing my hands, I leave the bathroom and find Frankie waiting.

"Did you just throw up?" she asks.

I nod.

She hands me a pack of mints from her purse. "Thank you."

"For what? I didn't do anything."

"You didn't leave me even though you're obviously deathly afraid of needles. You stayed, and we did it together."

Trying to play it off, I shrug. "I thought you'd kick my ass if I left."

Her shoulders are free of the tension that usually fills them. "Still, it means a lot to me. And I'm sorry about giving you so much shit about Gumdrop. I know you were trying to help."

Are we actually standing in the middle of a veterinarian office and having a civil conversation? I'd better go buy a lottery ticket because my luck is sure to run out soon.

CHAPTER TWELVE

Frankie

*J*pick up Jolie from school since Sandy has to work late. The minute she walks out of the building, it's clear something is wrong. She's strung tight and walking fast, determined to reach me, her backpack swinging from side to side. I bend down to get a hug, but Jolie stops right in front of me.

"How was your day?" I ask.

"Where's Gumdrop?"

"He's at Ink Envy with Jax. What's going on?"

She looks behind her and I follow her vision to a little girl who's always talking to her mom whenever I see her. She's got blonde pigtails and is dressed like she lives on the other side of town. The rich side. They probably belong to the country club.

I stand and grab Jolie's hand. "Let's go."

But Jolie tugs her hand free. "Mommy."

"What?" I ask.

She looks back again. "That's Annabelle. Her parents are doing the snowman building contest in the gazebo this weekend."

"Okay…"

"She asked if I was going."

"And?" *Please tell me you told her no.* I cannot build a snowman this weekend, and I've already been monopolizing everyone's schedule.

"I told her we were. Then she told me that her dad is an engineer, so she's going to win."

I look at the girl as she's about to walk by us, and she says, "Bye, Jolie, see you tomorrow."

The mom smiles, but the girl is definitely being sarcastic.

"Honey, I don't think I can do it. This weekend is hard."

Jolie slams one foot on the concrete and crosses both arms. "We can never do anything fun. You always have to work."

Then she walks in front of me and I follow, giving her time to cool off. When we enter Ink Envy, she stomps over to the chairs, takes off her coat and throws it down, then pulls out her notebook.

"Jolie," I say, waiting for her to look up.

She does, and I point at the jacket. She slides off the chair, walks over, and picks up her jacket. Then she hangs it on the last hook of the coat hanger since it's the only one she can reach. She stomps back over to where she was sitting.

Everyone's staring at us because this is not Jolie's usual behavior. At least not when they're around her. She's usually happy here, so I'm the only one who sees this side of her. I don't even have the heart to be upset about her reaction. I get it. I do. I do work a lot, but that's because we have a lot of expenses. Especially now that I have to pay a lawyer.

"What's up?" Dylan asks, looking up from the tattoo he's working on.

Jax is busy with a tattoo, but I can tell his attention is focused on our conversation. Lyle is holding Gumdrop, and it speaks volumes that Jolie didn't immediately run over to him when we came in.

I sit in my chair, my client due in ten minutes. "Jolie's in a mood."

"What's up, Jolie?" Dylan asks.

"Nothing." She crosses her arms and huffs.

"You're not going to tell them?" I say.

Her eyes narrow at me just like the other night when I told her she wasn't leaving the table until she ate her broccoli. "No."

"Okay, I'll tell them then."

I turn to them, but my eye catches on Jax's tattoo. It's stunning and I know he drew it, which grabs me even more. He wipes the client's skin and looks up at me, so I try to act as if I'm not gawking. He's so talented. He shouldn't be in Cliffton Heights. Hennessy was right about that much.

"No, I will. You'll make me sound dumb," Jolie says.

I hold out my hand as she crawls over to the chairs that have their backs to the stations and peers over them. "I wouldn't have, but by all means."

"My friend Annabelle is always saying how her parents go to all these places. For Christmas, she was on a beach with palm trees. Now they're doing the snowman competition by the gazebo this weekend."

I meet Dylan's gaze, and he sighs, understanding. I already went over my schedule with him, so he knows I'm almost completely booked. But after Christmas, I needed a busy weekend to pay it all off. Plus, Mr. Holder hasn't cashed my check yet, and I need to make sure there's enough in there for it to clear. I really need to call him about that. Last time we spoke, he told me that it must've been the holidays delaying things at the bank, but he knew I was good for the money.

"Mommy says we can't do it because she has to work. She's always working. And Santa brought me Gumdrop instead of..." Jolie stops talking.

All of us wait to see if she'll reveal what was in the letter.

"What's that, sweetie?" I ask.

She looks at Jax, then down at the floor. "Nothing."

My heart beats rapidly and disappointment weighs heavily on my shoulders. Talk about mommy guilt.

"Is this the same Annabelle who told you she rode an ostrich in Australia this summer?" Jax asks, and Lyle laughs. I forgot about that story.

"Yeah," Jolie answers.

Jax looks at Dylan over his shoulder and I know what's happening. I can almost read the silent conversation between them.

"No, you don't," I warn.

They both smirk and look at Jolie.

"We've got you. Where do we sign up?" Dylan is the one who says it, but I know Jax is on board.

"Really?" Jolie screeches, a huge smile on her face. "Both of you will help me?"

They look at one another again and nod. "Yep."

"Yay! Mommy, can I go next door?"

I chuckle at her quick change of mood since she got what she wanted.

Lyle puts Gumdrop down in his bed that Jax bought for him. "I'll walk her over."

"Thanks, Lyle."

After they're gone, I ignore the client in Dylan's chair. "You guys can't always pick up and change plans because she wants something."

They share another look then both smirk at me. "Yes, we can," they say in unison.

I blow out a breath. "You guys are busy this weekend too."

"I'm still appointment only, and I'm mostly only taking regulars right now," Jax says. That explains why his head has been more buried in his notebook than tattooing someone lately.

"And you?" I ask Dylan.

"Well, every time Rian sees me with Jolie, it earns me points."

I roll my eyes. "You're using my daughter to get laid?"

He looks guilty for a second then points at his client. "I need to pay attention." He looks away from me and gets back to work.

Chickenshit.

"Seriously, this Annabelle needs to get what she deserves." Jax sets his tattoo gun down for a minute and locks his gaze with mine.

"Let's remember she's a five-year-old."

"Five-year-olds can be assholes too. Usually trickles down the apple tree," Jax says.

I shake my head and sit down, pulling out the sketch for my client. Then I realize there's one thing I forgot to say.

"Hey, Jax?" I say, looking at him.

"Thanks."

He winks and smiles at me, and my stomach flips. What the hell was that? My stomach doesn't flip for Jax. It's never flipped for anyone.

On Saturday, I walk into the Rooftop Apartments where everyone lives. Sure enough, there's a sign by the mailboxes saying an apartment on the floor below everyone is for rent. Two bedroom, one bath.

Jolie and I step into the elevator, and for the first time, I wonder how nice it might be if we lived here. Then again, I've always felt like the one who drags her kid along and brings down the fun in their group. Still, they all treat Jolie like their adored niece or something, and there's no way I could ever thank them all enough for helping me with her. Especially since Michael doesn't care.

I knock on Dylan's apartment door, and he tells me to come in. As usual, their door is unlocked, so we walk in. He and Jax are at the kitchen table, looking down at a laptop.

"I think we have to do a mixture of food dye and water," Jax says.

Jolie walks up and slides onto a kitchen chair, leaning forward with her chin in her palm, enthralled by what they're talking about.

I place the canvas bag in my hand near the front door. "I brought a bag of snowman things, like a carrot and a scarf and—"

"Oh, we're not doing a boring snowman," Dylan says. "Our snowman is gonna be badass."

Rian comes out from the bedroom in her Sweet Infusion T-shirt and jeans. I know Kamea has been helping her more and more, and I wonder if she opened for Rian this morning. "Don't even bother, the two have been at this all night." She pulls her hair up into a ponytail, walking over to Jolie, then hugs her.

Jolie hugs her back fiercely.

"Are you excited? Make sure they include you, okay?" She runs her hand down Jolie's hair.

"She's included. What do you think the snowman would want? Tribal or skull?" Jax asks.

Jolie laughs. "We have to name him." As though she just

97

remembered, she perks up and looks out on the balcony. "I gotta go say hi to Earl."

"Oh, take Gumdrop with you so he can go to the bathroom." I hand her the puppy, and Winston waddles out behind them. I walk up to the table to find some sketches, mixtures of bottles, and an airbrush. They really are taking things too far. "Thanks for doing this. Remember, it's a family event."

"Oh, and here I was going to make the carrot his dick." Jax shakes his head.

"I meant more that I know you feel this protectiveness over Jolie, but we're not in competition with Annabelle and her family. You know that, right?"

Rian laughs, pouring a to-go cup of coffee. "Should've told them that yesterday."

"If you only lived here." Dylan glances up with a smirk.

"Live here?" Jax asks.

"The apartment for rent downstairs," Dylan fills him in.

Jax nods. "You might have some competition. I heard a detective and his girlfriend are thinking about moving in there."

Dylan and Rian stare at him in disbelief.

"I thought they wanted to stay with you?" Dylan asks.

Jax shrugs. "Knox brought it up casually. But you know if they move out, you can always move in." Jax winks at me, and his gaze drifts quickly over my body.

I resist the urge to shiver under his attention, and I refuse to revisit the night we were together in my thoughts. Not in front of him anyway.

"And one of you end up in a body bag?" Dylan laughs. "I like my peaceful floor, other than Seth's loud fucking."

"It is horrendous. He sounds like a hurt llama or something," Rian chimes in.

"Well, I wasn't going to take it anyway. We're only seven

blocks from here." I try to pretend I wasn't thinking of how nice it would be to live in this building right before I came up here. And they're right that although Jax and I have found common ground recently, for us to live so close to each other might ruin whatever friendship we've formed.

"Want a coffee?" Rian asks.

"No, I'll have one at the shop. I'm going to say goodbye to Jolie."

I walk through their apartment, seeing new pictures of Rian and Dylan on tables and walls. They've really built their life together in the short time they've been a couple. I'd be lying if I said I wasn't a little envious. Even when Michael and I were together, I'm not sure I ever framed a picture of us. We were too busy surviving. Not that I'm not happy for Dylan and Rian. They deserve all the happiness they've found.

"I'm leaving, so I'll see you later. Don't let the boys do anything crazy." I hold out my arms.

Jolie hugs me, kissing me on the cheek. "Mommy, Winston peed on Earl." She glares at Winston.

"Well, Earl's a tree, I think he's probably used to it."

She shakes her head. I pick up Gumdrop to bring him in.

"Bye, Earl." Jolie waves and goes back inside.

Winston follows me in. Rian's already got her coat on and kissing Dylan goodbye. I stand there awkwardly with Jax as they tell each other how much they love one another and say how much they'll miss each other.

"It's, like, eight hours," Jax says.

Rian waves at Jax while they kiss one last time. Once Rian and Dylan are away from one another, I try to act unfazed by their love.

"Be good, boys," I say, walking out with Rian.

"You know one of them might end up at the police station today?" Rian laughs as she hits the elevator button.

"Hopefully, Knox is on duty." We step inside.

"It's a shame about the apartment. I was hoping you'd move in. Dylan said he's been trying to convince you."

I shrug. "I guess it just wasn't meant to be."

She smiles. "Maybe another one will come up."

"Maybe." I shrug as if I don't care, but truth is, I'd love to live in this building with people who love my daughter more than her actual father does.

CHAPTER THIRTEEN

Jax

*D*ylan signs us up on the sheet, and we head over to our designated spot.

"I can't believe this is an actual thing. Could you imagine doing this when we were growing up?" I ask with Jolie's hand in mine because damn, there are so many people here.

"I'm pretty sure every snowman would've been holding a bottle of alcohol or they'd be smoking something."

We walk past the other families who have already started their snowmen, rolling the snow into big balls. Jolie's footsteps slow while she inspects everyone else's work. Once we reach our designated spot, I see that they've pushed snow into the spots so everyone would have enough. I swear this is next level *Leave it to Beaver* shit.

"*Jolie!*" A girl runs over, looking as if she's about to go on a ski trip in her matching pink snowsuit, hat, and gloves.

"Hey, Annabelle," Jolie says.

Dylan glances at me, and we share a look to say *"there's our competition."* No matter what Frankie said, we have to beat these people.

"We already started." Annabelle points, and I follow the direction of her finger to a couple arguing over the size of the snowballs. "My mom says my dad needs bigger balls and he says they're fine."

Dylan laughs but clears his throat immediately.

"You definitely want big balls," I say. "Introduce us to your friends, Jolie."

"This is Annabelle. Annabelle, this is Jax and Dylan."

"Are you her dads?" she asks.

"We're her uncles," Dylan chimes in. "Her dad couldn't be here, and her mom had to work."

"Oh…" Annabelle glances at her parents. Her mom is trying to push through the snow to make their bottom ball larger. "I better go. Good luck," she says and runs off.

Jolie's whole demeanor changes once her friend is gone. She's not nearly as excited as she was when we came over here.

"Come on, Dylan can't roll the ball himself." I nudge her, and Jolie rolls the smaller ball.

We work for an hour to get the balls the right size and to get them on top of one another without falling over. She should be happy it's Dylan and me because this shit is heavy. I catch Jolie glancing at Annabelle sometimes, and every time I look, her parents are arguing. Another reason Jolie should be happy it's Dylan and me here.

"Mommy gave me a scarf." Jolie pulls it out of the bag Frankie left.

"I'm going to find somewhere to plug in this extension cord." Dylan disappears.

Jolie sits on the ground, playing with the snow in her mittens. She glances at the people around us. Carrots, charcoal, top hats, and scarves all adorn their snowmen. The most original one is someone who put on their favorite sports team gear and another who made little snowmen to go with the big snowman.

Her nose scrunches up. "Different?"

I sit down with her, my ass freezing. "Different is another word for unique, and it's good to be unique."

She looks over at Annabelle who is putting that beige, black, and red plaid pattern I see on every rich woman in town on their snowman. "I don't like being different."

I nudge her leg. "How are you different?"

She shrugs, and my heart squeezes. Today was supposed to be fun. She should be smiling and happy. That's why I rearranged my schedule and canceled people who booked me two months ago.

Jolie says, "I don't have a dad."

"You do have a dad."

"Not a dad like that." She glares at Annabelle.

"True, but you have Dylan and me. I think that's a little better than just one dad." I act offended, and she laughs. "Want to know something?"

"What?"

I pack a snowball and start on another one. "I don't have a dad or a mom."

Her eyes widen. "Really? Why not?"

I shrug. "That's a long story, but I grew up okay, right?"

She smiles and nods in triple time.

"And you want to know another thing?"

"What?"

I hand her the snowball I made. "Dylan doesn't either. And he's pretty cool too, right?"

She nods.

"You're young and you might not understand this now,

but family doesn't have to mean that you share blood with them. Sometimes family are the friends you choose."

"Share blood?" Her forehead crinkles.

Shit, I have no idea how to talk to a five-year-old who just wants to be like every other kid—have a dad and a mom, live in a house with a yard, and have a dog to chase. I was there once myself, wanting all the same things.

"Scratch that. Everyone is dealt cards in life. Some people get both parents, some get mommies, some get daddies, some get none. But you make the most of what you do have, and you need to be grateful for what you were given."

Annabelle's parents' arguing grows louder. A reminder that not every relationship is perfect no matter how it might appear at first glance.

"Your mommy is pretty awesome, isn't she?"

Jolie nods. "Yeah."

"And because of her, you know all of us. And we're the coolest, right?"

She giggles and nods. "Yeah."

"I mean, Rian bakes with you, Knox lets you play with his handcuffs, Kamea made you that T-shirt you wanted, Seth lets you play with his camera, Blanca made you famous on her blog, and then there's me—I let you do all the stuff your real parent wouldn't." I wink at her, and she nods. "I bet a lot of your friends don't have that much. And you have Grandma Sandy too. A lot of people have grandparents who live far away, and they never see them."

She copies what I'm doing with the snowball and we end up having a good size stack in front of us.

"So try to think about what you do have, not what you don't, and you'll be a lot happier."

She stands and her small arms wrap around my neck, squeezing tight.

"What was that for?" I chuckle.

"For being you. I love you, Jax."

Dylan rounds our snowman and stops in his tracks, his eyebrows flying up to the edge of his knit cap.

"Thanks for being you, because you know I only hang out with the coolest people," I say.

She laughs and dislodges herself from me. "Dylan!" She gives him a hug.

I'm thankful for the reprieve because I need a moment after her undeserved declaration of love. Just hearing the words from her mouth makes me want to deserve them.

WE'RE FINISHING up the snowman and I can't even argue with Dylan about his drive to get the full sleeve tattoo perfect. Most families are sitting around drinking hot chocolate and eating cookies. Jolie and I are trying to get the disposable gloves on the arms made out of branches.

"How come it's a snowman?" Jolie asks.

Dylan stops what he's doing to look at her.

"There are no girls." Her gaze scatters along all the finished snowmen.

Dylan looks at me. I pull my phone out of my pocket because we're totally on the same wavelength.

"Let's make a snowwoman then?" I ask Jolie.

Her eyes light up and she looks at the tattoo. "Mommy. The snowwoman could be Mommy."

Dylan nods. "Definitely. But everything we brought is more for a man."

"I'm calling reinforcements," I say, looking at my phone and typing away.

Jolie and I finally get the disposable gloves on after the branches breaking through them ten times. Dylan's finished with the full sleeve, making some colors more feminine than we had originally planned. We're just about done when Annabelle walks over with her mom.

"Oh, this is unique," her mom says.

I look at Jolie and wink.

The mom's eyes fall over Dylan and me as though she'd like a scoop of whatever we're serving. She's the epitome of a squeaky clean rich girl wanting to see what's on the other side of the tracks. I've seen it and taken advantage of it more than I'd care to admit.

"It's my mommy," Jolie says.

"Really?" Annabelle asks, her face twisted in disgust.

"Yeah, because my mommy is a tattoo artist." Jolie's sweet smile makes my chest warm.

"Oh yes, do you guys work at that Ink Envy?" the mom asks.

Dylan rolls his eyes so that I'm the only one that can see.

"We do," I say.

"I keep telling my friends we should all go in and get matching ones. Do you do parties?"

"Parties?" I tilt my head.

"Yes, like I rent the place out, we all get tattoos and drink wine, have some laughs and a good time." She eyes me over the rim of her hot chocolate cup as though I'm involved in the "have a good time" part.

"We never have before, but I guess we could. Unfortunately, Jolie's mom, Frankie, and Jax here are by appointment only usually. They're in high demand," Dylan says, putting away his airbrush.

"I bet you're in high demand." She raises her eyebrows at me.

Even I'm creeped out. Good thing Frankie and Rian walk up just in time.

"Mommy!" Jolie screeches and tugs on her hand.

Frankie looks toward where we're talking with

Annabelle's mom but allows herself to be distracted by the snowwoman.

"It's you," Jolie declares.

"Me?"

Rian laughs, and Dylan kisses her hello.

Annabelle's mom doesn't miss their interaction, frowning a bit. "You own Sweet Infusion, right?" She points at Rian.

Rian dislodges herself from Dylan, giggling. "I do."

"You have the best chocolate cake. I got it for Annabelle's birthday party and all the kids loved it."

"Oh, I remember. Two weeks ago, right?" Rian smiles. "Thank you so much."

As my head volleys between them, I see Jolie's smile fade. I don't remember mention of a birthday party that Jolie went to a couple of weeks ago.

"Hi, I'm Frankie, Jolie's mom." Frankie steps up to my side and puts out her hand. "Jolie talks about Annabelle a lot."

The mom shakes Frankie's hand and smiles, but it doesn't even reach her cheeks, let alone reach her eyes. "Nice to meet you. I see you pick her up sometimes. Otherwise it's her nanny?"

My forehead scrunches. Do we look like nanny people?

"Oh, that's her grandma," Frankie says.

"That's sweet. I'm not sure we could get Annabelle's grandmother out from all her charity work to pick her up."

Frankie nods, her smile not genuine either.

Annabelle walks over to Jolie and the two talk about the other snowmen. I can tell that Jolie is upset now that she's realized she wasn't invited to Annabelle's birthday party.

"We should get going. I'll definitely keep that booking in mind. Are there private rooms if I want a tattoo in a more... discreet spot?" she asks while eye-fucking me.

Frankie makes that sound she does when she's annoyed. I put my arm around her waist and tug her closer. At first she fights it, trying to lean the opposite way, but my hand locks on her hip.

"Sure thing. But Frankie would have to do that. She's pretty protective of me doing those types of tattoos even though I tell her all the time she's the only one for me."

Frankie's head whips in my direction and I press my lips to hers. Surprisingly, she doesn't push me away. My lips tingle with the urge to deepen our kiss, but we're in public.

"Oh, right. Well, good luck. Hope your snowwoman comes in second—after us, of course." She laughs. "Annabelle!" she yells and walks away.

Once they're gone, I let Frankie go.

"What was that?" she asks.

"I didn't like the way she acted like she was better than you. Plus Annabelle clearly had a birthday party and Jolie wasn't invited."

Frankie's eyebrows rise. "So you thought acting like we're a couple was proof of what exactly?"

I'm not going to be arrogant and say I did it because Annabelle's mom clearly wanted me. I wanted to stick it to her and stop her from looking down at Frankie and Jolie.

"Cute display, Jax. I'd almost say you were being protective." Rian's eyes light up.

Oh no. I know that look. That's the love glow Rian gets when she thinks something is romantic.

I'm just as struck as Frankie, because normally, I wouldn't give a shit if some snooty woman looked down on us. What's happening to me?

CHAPTER FOURTEEN

Frankie

*S*andy's watching Jolie because Knox and Kamea want to host a game night. I could use a night off of momming, but I'm not sure I could use it with Jax. Ever since the snowman competition a week ago, I can't help but think about what it would be like if we *were* a couple.

I brought Gumdrop with me since I didn't want to hand that responsibility off to Sandy too, so I told Jolie Gumdrop needed a night with his daddy. When I knock on the door, Kamea answers.

"Hey, Frankie," she says, stepping aside and letting me in.

"Have you hidden all your shoes? Because Gumdrop is still chewing things like crazy." I might sound exasperated, but this little guy has wormed his way into my heart.

"I think Jax said he picked something up to help with that."

Just as she's about to show me something on the counter,

Jax comes out of his room. He sits on the floor and claps his hands, smiling. "Gumdrop!"

I put the puppy down and he waddles right over to Jax and crawls into his lap. Jax stands with Gumdrop in his arms. My ovaries let out a big sigh.

"This is what he picked up." Kamea hands me a bottle.

"It's some kind of bitter apple taste. You spray it everywhere and it's supposed to help. I got us each a bottle," Jax says.

I put the bottle in my purse. "Thank you. How much do I owe you?"

Gumdrop whines, so Jax puts him down on the floor.

"Nothing. It's a co-parent gift." He waves me off. "I also got some training treats. I thought about the obedience training and I've been looking things up online. I think I can do it, so we don't have to pay someone else."

"Really?" I'm skeptical.

He nods. "I mean, it would be better if I was with him full time, but I'll do what I can at the shop and when I have him."

"Okay." Then I remember what Jax mentioned before. "Kamea, are you and Knox moving downstairs?"

She looks at Jax, and he sighs. "Yeah, they're leaving me."

"Now you have the place to yourself." I smile, trying not to think about how that gives Jax the freedom to bring his hookups here as he pleases.

He nods. "Thankfully. Now I can pee in the morning without listening to the groaning."

"Because he doesn't shut the door." Kamea laughs and shakes her head.

The apartment door opens and Seth bounces in. "Let's play! Just a warning that I'm a champion at everything I do."

Evan comes in behind him, shaking her head.

Seth kisses my cheeks. "I heard I missed quite the snow-woman. Spitting image of you, huh?"

"I guess so." I hug him and pat his shoulder. "Hey, Evan."

"Hey, Frankie. Where's the little guy?"

Jax and I both look at one another. Shit, quiet is never good when a puppy is involved. We both look through the apartment. How could something small get away? After looking under the couch and chairs and in the bathroom, I find Gumdrop in Jax's room, chewing on his boots. He's already got the top chewed off and is working his way down.

"No, Gumdrop!" I grab the boot.

Jax comes in and his shoulders sink as he looks at one of his new boots that is now a mauled piece of leather.

"You gotta be fucking kidding me," he says, coming closer to inspect the boot in my hand.

My heart races and I brace myself for his anger, grabbing Gumdrop before Jax can. Jax stops his approach and looks at me for a moment before slowly taking Gumdrop from my arms. I stare intently at Jax, my breath lodged in my throat.

Jax puts his finger in Gumdrop's face. "Bad dog, no chewing. Come on, I got you a chew toy for this kind of thing."

He walks out with Gumdrop and the breath I was holding finally releases. I stay there for a minute, trying to collect myself. Jax returns, putting Gumdrop down with a chew bone he must have bought at the store.

"I read that you have to say no, then show them an item they can chew." He picks up his boot. "Damn, these were expensive." He throws everything on the floor in the closet and shuts the door. "They said the chewing phase is a long one, so get prepared to lose stuff."

"You're not mad?" I ask, stepping toward the door.

"Yeah, I'm pissed. Like I said, those were expensive, but what can I do?" He shrugs.

I could tell him what Michael might have done.

Jax stops before we leave his room, barricading me with

his arms on the frame of the door. "We're not all assholes. You can trust me, Frankie."

He holds my gaze for a moment, then pushes off the frame and joins his friends. But my feet feel as if they're stuck in cement. I never thought Michael's reactions to things made that much of a lasting impression on me, but I was clearly afraid that Jax was going to hurt the dog. That's not fair to Jax, because he's never shown me that he has a crazy temper.

God help me. I press my hand to my stomach to stop the hummingbirds from flapping their wings when I think about being with Jax again. But I'm pretty sure I'm losing the battle within myself of not wanting him.

I SHOULD'VE KNOWN this group of friends wouldn't play normal games like Charades or Pictionary. We end up playing 5 Second Rule Uncensored, where you have to name three things that relate to the topic on the card. Jax picks up a card to ask me, and Sierra's got the timer in her hand, ready to turn it over. I've never been good at thinking fast.

"Three erogenous zones?" Jax asks me with a wicked grin because he already knows some of mine.

"Oh, I love this one," Blanca says.

"You want to know Frankie's erogenous zones?" Ethan asks her.

They all laugh.

"Hello? Maybe new places you haven't discovered," she says, and Sierra raises her hand for a high five.

"Babe, I've discovered your entire body," Ethan says. "Believe me, we've found them all. But if you want to ditch this party and see if we can find a new one, you know I'm game."

"Better do it before you're an old married couple," Seth says.

"Speaking of which, I need the RSVP from you two." Blanca wiggles her fingers between Jax and me.

Neither of us says anything. The only reason I haven't RSVPed is because I have to fill out whether I'm bringing a guest or not. The thought of going to a wedding by myself sounds about as pleasant as putting a staple in my eye.

"I'll get it in the mail," I say.

"Okay, enough talk! Let's get to the game," Jax distracts everyone.

"Owens, why do you want to know Frankie's erogenous zones so badly?" Seth asks, and Jax rolls his eyes.

"Ready, set, go." Sierra flips the timer.

"Okay, um, back of the neck, nipples, and um… my inner thighs."

"Good ones. I love the collarbone," Sierra says.

"I love my neck and shoulders." Rian closes her eyes as if Dylan's kissing her there right now.

And it's the first time I realize that when playing this game, they're all going home horny with someone to satisfy them. I'm going home horny to my vibrator that doesn't kiss any of my erogenous zones.

"Me too." Blanca falls to the back of the couch.

Ethan stares at her as though he doesn't know what she's talking about. "I just did that the other day and you pushed me away so hard I have a bruise on my hip from hitting the counter."

"I was working, and my mind was focused on that. You pick all the wrong times to do that."

"Okay, maybe you want to write me down a schedule of when I should approach you and when I should leave you alone?" There's a bitterness in Ethan's tone and I'm not the only one who hears it.

"Relax, love birds. After the wedding, you can screw one another senseless without the pressure of your upcoming nuptials." Rian smiles at them.

"That's why I don't do commitment," Jax says.

I whip my head in his direction. I hate that persona he puts on sometimes. "Why? Because the woman doesn't bow down and give you a blow job every time you unbutton your pants?"

He raises his hands. "Hey now, let's not involve ourselves in their drama."

"You did when you made that ridiculous commitment comment."

"What's ridiculous about it?" His forehead wrinkles.

A few people get up to get a new drink and Evan refills the chips.

"Maybe men should get a badge to wear around that says, 'Commitment scares me, you've been warned.'"

Kamea laughs and puts up her hand for me to high five.

"Why are you laughing? I committed right away," Knox says.

"Because I agree with her. Not everything has to do with you, Knox." She shakes her head at him.

"If I wore that badge, ten times the amount of women would be attracted to me," Jax says. "Women like to think they can be the ones to change a man's mind. But the truth is, you can't flip a man who doesn't want commitment."

Rian raises her hand. "I beg to differ."

Dylan kisses her shoulder. "Me too."

"Please, Phillips was never the no-commitment guy. He just needed his priorities straightened out." Jax looks around the room. "As the only one here who believes that being with one person for the rest of your life is a crock of shit, let me tell you, men like that don't change."

I head to the kitchen to get away from him. I wish I could

hide my upset feelings because why do I even care if that's what Jax thinks? "Then die alone."

"You can say what you will, but I tell the women right off the bat. They can't blame me if they put on rose-colored glasses and get attached."

"Jax..." Rian's tone is one of warning. "What's with you?"

"I'm just saying, some of us are too screwed up to have a serious relationship."

"That's not true." Sierra raises her finger. "Dylan was really screwed up and look at our Prince Charming now." She pinches his cheeks, and Dylan smacks her hand away.

"Okay, enough about me. Can we just play the game?" Jax says.

"Yes, let's play a drinking game." Adrian raises the game they brought.

"Sure, add alcohol to this group of angry people. Great idea." Seth shakes his head, falling back into the couch.

"Drinking game? I'm in." I sit back down between Rian and Jax. "This should be right up your alley." I grab the Do or Drink game that Adrian held, pick up a card, and look at Jax. "Ready, Don Juan?"

"Always," he says before sipping his beer.

"'Dick card.' Everyone with a dick, drink up." I raise my eyebrows in challenge to Jax, but the next card is the brunette card and Blanca and I have to drink.

By the time my turn comes around again, I'm more than buzzed. Soon my ass is close to Jax's hand, our thighs are touching, and his smell is hypnotizing me. Damn alcohol and its power to make you forget why you were pissed off.

The game disperses after only a few rounds. Seth turns on music, and all the girls rush to the center of the room as if there's a dance floor. Slowly, one by one, each woman entices her guy to join her, grinding their hips in a slow dirty dancing move.

At some point, I look around and realize Jax and I are the only ones not coupled up. He's sitting on the couch, legs spread wide, sipping his beer, eyes on me. My breath lodges in my throat. How can he spout all that shit about commitment when he's more than committed to my daughter and Gumdrop than even Jolie's father is? It's not a commitment to me, but it still says something about the man.

But I push all that out of my mind because he's looking good tonight and all that sex talk has me hot and bothered. So I walk toward Jax, swaying my hips, biting my lip, ready to straddle him—until I trip over the corner of the coffee table and stumble head-first into his crotch. I pick my head up to look at him, and he tucks a strand of hair behind my ear. Am I crazy for thinking he's wrong about the commitment thing? Probably, but tonight, I don't care either way.

Just as I'm about to rise up on my feet, a queasiness turns my stomach inside out and I throw up all over Jax's lap.

Smooth, Frankie. Real smooth.

CHAPTER FIFTEEN

Jax

"*I*'m soooo sorrrrry," Frankie slurs.

All of our friends stare at me in horror, wondering how I'll react. What is with people thinking I have some temper? It pisses me off.

"Party's over," I say.

Rian and Bianca walk over to either side of Frankie.

"Come on, let's get you cleaned up," Rian says.

"I've got her, just move the party over to your place," I tell Rian.

She steps back for a moment. "We can handle this."

"So can I."

"Are you sure? We're all here." Kamea steps forward.

"I'm positive." I slide to the side and gently place Frankie's head on the sofa.

Our friends trust me enough to file out of the apartment, Rian and Kamea lingering. "If you need us…"

"Go."

It's not that I don't want their help. I mean, who wants to clean up puke all by themselves? No one. But Frankie deserves to not have everyone see her in this state. I know she'd hate it if they did. She's the most in control of her life, the most mature out of all of us. She'll be embarrassed enough tomorrow without having them further witness this mess.

"This isn't gonna be pretty," I murmur to her after everyone leaves.

I unbutton my pants and lower them to the floor, then I strip my shirt carefully to keep the puke from going everywhere. In my boxers, I take a garbage bag and throw away the clothes. Guess I'll be shopping for new boots, new jeans, and a new T-shirt now.

I turn on the shower to warm up the water and head back to get Frankie. Her face has puke on it and it's in her hair. I stare at her for a moment, resting on the couch and looking so innocent, without that chip that's usually prominently displayed on her shoulder. She hasn't had the easiest life in the past few years. Although I know nothing of how she grew up, the last few years would've broken a lesser woman, but she's still so tough and strong.

"We're going to take a shower," I say.

She groans and picks up her head. "I'm so sorry. I didn't plan on drinking that much."

"That's apparent."

I hold her up the majority of the trip to the bathroom, but we get there, nonetheless.

"Frankie?" I say, waiting for her to stop staring at the floor and look at me. "Are you okay if I take off your clothes? It's just to get you in the shower."

She nods. "You already saw me naked." Her head circles to the other side.

"Don't remind me of that right now." I glance down at myself since I only have my boxer briefs between us. "Okay, sit on the toilet."

I position her and strip off her socks, revealing the cutest red-painted toes. She wiggles them as though she's ticklish, and I wonder what would happen if we weren't in this situation and I tickled her. Would she squirm until I caught her?

Then comes the hard part—her shirt. I grab the hem and pull it up, keeping the vomit from getting more on her than it is. "Are you committed to this shirt?"

She shrugs.

I get the shirt off and see that she's wearing a see-through bra. She's got to be kidding me. My boxers tent and I attempt to hide my growing erection.

"Now we're going to stand." I hold her up and place her hands on the towel rack. "Hold on to this."

I unbutton her jeans and slide them down her legs, her ass right in my face with a matching pair of see-through panties.

Fuck, kill me now.

I undo her bra from the back, and it falls forward, hanging off her shoulders. She moves one arm then the other, and the bra falls to the floor like one of those helicopter leaves I played with when I was younger.

I hook my fingers on either side of her panties and close my eyes, then slide them over her ass and down her legs. She's so damn hot and has no idea. I'd do about anything just to kiss her back tattoo right now.

"Now I have to go in the shower with you, okay?" I don't trust her not to slip and fall.

"Sure." She turns around and her arms move over my shoulders, then she breathes right in my face and I gag. She covers her mouth. "Sorry."

I hate her being apologetic right now. She has no idea

what it's like to be taken care of and I kind of like that I'm the one who gets to do it. And it has nothing to do with her being naked right now.

I step into the shower first, holding her up, and get her under the stream of water. I'm not sure if it's the fresh water or what, but she seems more alert after I rinse all the vomit off of her, so I can wash her hair. She sighs as I work Kamea's shampoo through her hair then condition it. But I lather up her body with my soap because I wouldn't mind her smelling me on herself, as sick as that probably is. I avoid all her sexual parts because I don't want her looking back on this and thinking I did it for some cheap thrill.

Once she's all cleaned up, she looks as though it took every ounce of energy she had to take a shower. So I guide her to step out and hold on to the towel rack until I can step out. After grabbing a new towel from under the sink, I wrap her in it and pick her up to carry her to my room.

I lay her on my bed and grab two shirts and pairs of shorts—one for me and one for her. But when I turn toward the bed and see her lying there, I'm struck, as though she's supposed to be there, like she belongs.

Gumdrop jumps at my legs, but I can't take my eyes off of her. She's so beautiful and she deserves someone she can be like this with. Someone who will take care of her, not hurt her. Someone to share the burdens of everyday life with. A possessiveness spurs inside me, urging me to be that person.

I shake my head. "What the fuck am I even thinking?"

I dress her in my shirt and shorts, doing what I can not to look at her. I sit her up long enough to comb out her hair, then I put her to sleep on her side, tucking her into my bed. Picking up Gumdrop, I take him out to the living room and dress in the second pair of shorts and T-shirt I pulled out. Then I clean up everything before taking her clothes downstairs to the laundry room in the basement.

She's still passed out as I pull Gumdrop into my lap on the chair in the corner of my room and watch her to make sure she doesn't roll over. For the first time in my life, I think about what sharing a life with someone would be like, coming home to a woman like Frankie every night. It looks really nice in my crystal ball. Like something I might enjoy. And that thought terrifies me.

———

I'M DRINKING coffee the next morning while attempting to teach Gumdrop how to sit, using mini treats that wouldn't get me to sit on my ass for anyone, when Frankie makes an appearance. Damn, she looks better than I do in my clothes.

"So it wasn't a dream," she says.

"Did you see the aspirin and water I put on the nightstand?"

She nods and sits down next to me. "I just talked to Sandy. Thank you for calling her last night, and thanks for taking care of me."

I nod. "You're welcome. It happens."

She falls forward, her head in her hands. "I've never been more embarrassed."

I hold the treat for Gumdrop and nudge his butt down, then I give him a treat. "Surely you've been more embarrassed than just throwing up on someone."

She side-glances me and shakes her head.

"Then you need to get out more. Do more crazy shit," I say.

"I have a five-year-old. Getting drunk at a game night might be my limit of crazy shit. And now I will kindly refuse any other invitations."

I knock my shoulder with hers. "No, you won't. We've all had nights like that." I hold up the treat and again Gumdrop stares at me as if he has no idea what to do. I nudge his ass down again, say "Sit," then give him the treat.

Frankie laughs next to me. "I'd like him to stop chewing things and peeing everywhere before we get him to sit."

"He'll get there." I pick him up and pet him, giving him a break.

Frankie slides closer, and I smell my soap on her when she pets Gumdrop. Knowing my scent is on her brings some latent caveman tendency to the surface, making my dick twitch.

"You're really good with him," she says.

"Well, someone said he was half my responsibility. I can't have an asshole for a dog."

She laughs and why does it sound so different than it did weeks ago? Why is there an urge inside me to make her laugh again?

"I should get going." She pets Gumdrop one more time and stands.

"Your clothes are on the chair in my room."

I don't look to see her reaction, but she sighs. "You didn't have to wash them, but thank you so much."

"No problem," I mumble.

A second later, my bedroom door shuts.

Get yourself together, Jax. This isn't anything but a friendship forming. I'm not catching feelings. It's just the tornado we're in that keeps throwing us together. That has to be all it is—because if I have feelings for Frankie and I fuck it up, my entire life here in Cliffton Heights will be blown to smithereens.

She walks out of the bedroom a little later, dressed in her own clothes. "Do you want me to take Gumdrop?"

I shake my head. "Mind if I keep him for the day? I mean, if Jolie—"

"She'll be fine."

"I'll drop him off tonight."

"Sure." She opens the apartment door and stands in the hallway.

Blanca and Ethan walk past, and they're nice enough not to say anything to Frankie about her drunken incident last night.

"RSVPs, peeps!" Blanca points at both of us before they continue to the stairs. Those two always seem to be in a rush.

"I forgot about that," Frankie says.

"Me too."

"Maybe I'll take Lyle as my plus one. At least that way I'll have a date, but I won't have to worry about shaving my legs or anything."

I stretch my arms on the doorframe, chuckling until the memory of slipping her panties down her clean-shaven legs last night comes to mind.

"Yeah, I don't want to shave either, so how about…" I am a complete moron for doing this. It's only asking for trouble. "We go together. Saves Blanca and Ethan money."

"True, that would mean two place settings they wouldn't have to pay for," she says. "And you don't have to shave your legs."

"Yeah, I hate shaving." I pretend to run a hand down my hairy leg. "What do you say?"

She nods. "Sure. But I won't be drinking much. There will be no replay of last night."

"I kind of liked you all vulnerable and free," I say, my feelings slipping out like an idiot.

"Says the man who had to clean up my vomit. Did you shower me?" She lifts her arm to smell the back of her hand. "I smell like you."

"I didn't mind."

"Still… thank you." She steps back to leave, and I realize that I want to beg her to stay.

"You're welcome… again."

She smiles. Damn, she's gorgeous without makeup and her hair not done. "Bye." She waves and turns, but before she walks down the hallway to the elevator, she spins back around. "Jax?"

I lower my hands from the doorframe. "Yeah?"

"I think you underestimate yourself. You'd make someone really happy. Behind that commitment-phobe is a really good guy."

Before I can respond, she walks away. I hear the elevator ding its arrival, and I shut the door and close my eyes. Is this what's happened to all my friends? It can't be. I'm the foster kid whose perspective on life and love was screwed up from the beginning.

CHAPTER SIXTEEN

Frankie

A knock sounds on our apartment door and Jolie runs down the hall from her bedroom.

"Hold on." I wipe my hands on the dishcloth and look through the peephole since no one buzzed up. It's Jax with Gumdrop. I open the door.

"*Jax!*" Jolie yells and runs right into his legs.

"Hey." He looks at me as he pats her back.

"Let him in," I tell Jolie and she steps back, allowing him space to come in with Gumdrop.

He sets the dog on the floor, and Jolie follows Gumdrop as he gets reacquainted with all his stuff at our place.

"Something smells good," Jax says.

"Just spaghetti, nothing fancy." I head back into the kitchen to stir the sauce. "You're welcome to stay."

"Yeah, stay, Jax," Jolie says.

I knew she would. She loves Jax so much it scares me that

I'm setting us all up for failure. But having a positive male role model in her life can't be a bad thing, right?

In the past week since I threw up on him, things between us have felt different. We're nicer to one another and are having conversations without the constant digs on one another.

"Are you sure you have enough?" he asks.

"Yeah, I made a whole box and it's only us."

He comes into the kitchen, taking off his coat, and washes his hands. "Well then, put me to work."

I push him out of the kitchen. "Nope. I've got this. Consider it payback for last night."

"Stop feeling bad about that. You would've done the same for me." He sits at our small table. "Jolie, come here." She runs over to him and he hands her a small bag of treats. "Ask Gumdrop to sit."

She turns to find Gumdrop right behind her. "Sit, Gumdrop."

He actually does it.

"Now give him a treat," Jax says.

As she gives the dog a treat, Jolie's mouth falls open and she looks at me in astonishment. "He did it."

"Pretty cool. Way to go," I say to Jax with a smile.

"The chewing thing isn't getting much better unfortunately," he says.

"I heard it could be almost two years before he stops." At least that's what my client told me the other day, and he said he's had numerous dogs throughout his life.

"Great."

We sit as I stir the pasta and check the garlic bread in the oven. Jolie keeps telling Gumdrop to sit. It's weird how comfortable this situation feels.

When Jolie goes into the other room to play with the dog, Jax asks, "Have you heard from the lawyer?"

"We're at a standstill because he can't find Michael. He said that if Michael's gone without any contact for six months, things will go a lot easier in court. I'm not sure I want to wait that long... but hey, did he cash your check?" I ask.

"What?"

"He hasn't cashed my check, and I feel like he keeps making excuses about it. I've been waiting so I don't spend the money in the bank. But at this point, I wonder if he lost it."

"No it's not just you, he hasn't cashed mine either," he says.

My forehead wrinkles, but I feel slightly better about it. "Did you hear from him?"

He nods.

I rest the spoon on the holder and go to the table to sit with him. "Did he find your parents?"

He nods. "He thinks he found my mom."

My eyes widen. "Does she live locally?"

"Yeah, she has a permanent residence at a cemetery up in Southport."

"Oh." My shoulders fall. "She's already passed?"

He nods. "Turns out Momma fell in with the wrong crowd because she was an addict. No idea about my father. He's trying to turn up some relatives. Supposed to hear back in a week or so."

I grab his hand. "I'm sorry, Jax."

He shakes his head and shrugs. "It's fine. If he can find any family, I'll probably get the medical information I wanted. Same difference."

The sound of water spilling over on the stove has me out of my seat and rushing to the stove to lower the heat.

"Sorry," I say when I return, but he's shaking his head.

"I don't want to talk about it."

"Okay, well, if you could cut the garlic bread, I'll get the pasta ready and we'll eat."

I know that when I want to get my mind off something, I like to keep busy.

He cuts the bread as I drain the pasta. We move around the kitchen together, me handing him things since he doesn't know where anything is. Five minutes later, we're at the table like a real family and I have to remind myself that we're not. Jolie is telling Jax about a new friend, Isaiah, she's playing with at school.

"A boy?" Jax asks and eyes me.

"Yeah, and he's so nice. He has two mommies."

"Really?" He twirls his pasta.

"So I told him on Daddy Day that you'd pretend to be his daddy too. Okay?"

I choke on my pasta. She never told me that earlier when she was going on and on about her new friend at school.

"Sure, just hire me out for any kindergarteners who need me." Jax ruffles her hair, then he and Jolie bury their heads in their meals.

I twirl my pasta, wishing this pull on my heart would go away because one thing Jax has made clear is he isn't interested in any type of commitment. And when you have a five-year-old daughter, that's the first thing you need from a man.

JOLIE SWINDLES Jax to stay for a movie, and the three of us cuddle on the couch with her between us. Talk about breaking your heart—watch your daughter happy as a princess when the man she wants as her daddy sits down to watch a movie with her. It's heartbreakingly sweet.

As we watch the thief win the princess's heart, all I can think about are these feelings for Jax growing inside me. It's horrible that he'll never know his mother. I can only imagine how that must make him feel. I'm not close to my family at all, but they're there in Wisconsin should I wish to have a relationship with them—not that they want one with me. Being the black sheep of your family isn't the same as not having one. Is that what's making these feelings surface? Because sometimes he seems almost lonely and the motherly instinct in me wants to nurture him?

I could probably convince myself of that, but it would be a lie. I love Jax's sarcastic humor. Hell, the majority of the time we went rounds with our bickering, I felt this sexually charged energy between us, as if he could back me up to a wall and shut me up with a kiss. The way he is with Jolie is a completely opposite side. I'm not sure he even notices how good he is with her. It's like he doesn't see how much she looks up to him.

"Why is it that someone has to be poor and the other one rich?" Jax asks.

I look over to find Jolie's head tucked under his arm. She's asleep, nestled into his side. My ovaries are on high alert again. "How do you mean?"

"Think of all the movies. He's the thief and she's the princess who wants to get out of her castle, and she falls in love with him. Of course her father, the king, doesn't think he's worthy. Then you have Cinderella. She's got a wicked stepmother who locks her in the attic where she talks to mice."

"I'm oddly impressed that you know your fairy tales." I chuckle.

"I've had foster sisters my entire life. But seriously, in *Cinderella*, you have the prince who's searching out the woman who left a glass slipper and she turns out to have nothing? I mean, I think in reality, the prince takes all the girls who are vying for his affection."

I raise my eyebrows. "I'm going to need you to cover my daughter's ears while talking like that."

He chuckles. "Maybe it's the ones who don't get a fairy tale who are the most cynical that they exist."

"I could see that."

He looks down at Jolie. "Maybe I'm just bitter."

"Jolie told me what you said to her that day at the snowman competition. Ever think about taking your own advice?"

When she told me Jax told her to be thankful for what she has, she listed all of her friends, including everyone at the Rooftop Apartments.

"I'm thankful for my friends. Hopefully, your ex leaving doesn't affect Jolie too much." His eyes find mine through the glow of the television in the dark room. "I think I'm too messed up from my childhood to have a healthy relationship."

I don't respond because I almost think he's baiting me. Like he feels this thing between us too, but he's warning me not to expect anything because he's too damaged.

He shakes his head. "I don't know. I just hate fairy tales. I always relate to the damaged one who has to do all the growing. They aren't realistic."

"Would you rather the princess get her ass kicked by the drunk prince, so kids think that's normal behavior for people when they fall in love?"

I meant it as a joke, but I think my words hit too close to home because his lips tip down and his expression reads angry. "That's not reality either."

"Then what's reality?"

He shrugs. "Two people who have great sex and mistake lust for love. They marry, have a few kids. Raise the kids while they stop having sex or enjoying one another at all.

Then the kids grow up and they live the rest of their lives in bickering hell."

"Whoa, so all of our friends are on the path to hell, huh?"

He chuckles. "I've tried to warn every one of them."

I distinctly remember him talking Dylan into dating Rian.

I look down to make sure Jolie is still sleeping. "What about when bickering turns into make-up sex?"

"Eventually the make-up sex ends because she's not in the mood. Have you never seen this scenario in a movie?"

"Have you ever read a romance book?"

He chuckles. "Touché." He leans back, wiggling in his seat.

"If you're uncomfortable, I can take her to her room."

He shakes his head. "So tell me, when you meet someone you want to be with, how do you envision your life going?"

"First I have to find someone willing to take on Jolie and love her like his own."

He looks down at her and smiles. "She's easy. Hell, she thought she wanted me for her daddy. We really need to work on her taste. She can't be trying to find boys like me when she's a teenager. I'm sure whoever you're with won't be able to stop himself from loving her."

My heart is desperate to tell him, *maybe you're him.* But I don't because Jax clearly isn't ready for any of that. "After that, I'm simple. I just want a comfortable, peaceful life."

"House with a white picket fence?" he asks, arching one eyebrow.

I shake my head. "No, I don't even care if I live here the rest of my life. I just want a good life, a happy one. One where we're a team whether it be making dinner, or paying the bills, or raising a child. I just want someone on my team, someone as invested in our future as me. I think if I have that, the sex won't disappear. And I for one still think bickering can lead to great make-up sex."

"Because you're a woman and like to romanticize everything."

I point at him. "If you didn't have my daughter right now..." I press my lips together and shake my head at him, suppressing my smile.

"C'mon now. Don't forget that I know all your erogenous zones. Payback's a bitch."

"You only know three and what are you gonna do, leave me in a state of panting?"

"I guess you'll find out if you finish that sentence." He stretches and Jolie moves a bit. "Do you mind if I put her in bed?"

Hold on, ovaries, we're going for a joyride. "Do I mind not having to pick up my daughter's dead weight and carry her to bed? Have at it."

He manages to get out of her hold and picks her up, then carries her down the hall. I follow and watch him turn down the covers and place them back over her.

"Nightlight?" he whispers, pointing to the rainbow light on the wall near her bed.

I nod and he flicks it on. As he leaves the room, I want to grab him by his shirt and pull him toward me. Tell him he's got himself all wrong and he is a family man, just look at him. But I tried that with a different man before and all he brought with him was heartbreak. I can't risk Jolie's heart again. The next time has to be the real thing and whoever he is has to be fully invested in making it work.

CHAPTER SEVENTEEN

Jax

I crack my neck outside Frankie's apartment before I buzz up. The tie around my neck feels as if it's suffocating me. Most of our friends are in the wedding though, so I'm just thankful I don't have to wear a tuxedo.

"Hey, come on up," Frankie's voice comes through the speaker.

I take the elevator up and walk down the hall to find Jolie already in the hallway. She looks pretty in her silver dress with white tights and black shoes.

"Hey, shouldn't you be inside?" I pick her up and take her back in the apartment. "You look beautiful."

"The tights are itchy," she says.

I put her down when we get inside. Gumdrop's head peeks out from behind a corner and he comes over.

"Mommy says don't pet him, he'll get fur all over you."

"Mommy doesn't tell me what to do." I wink at her.

Frankie comes out and says, "Be careful, I swear he's losing his puppy coat or something."

I glance over to say something sarcastic, but any words lodge in my throat when I get a look at her. Holy shit, she's stunning.

A dark blue satin dress clings to all her curves and flows all the way to the floor. Her hair is swept to one side, and when she turns to grab something, I see that her tattooed back is shown off in all its glory. Nothing is more attractive to me than when a woman doesn't hide her ink but picks out something that makes the art an accessory to her outfit.

I stand, ignoring Gumdrop's whines. Frankie puts on her heels, making her only a couple inches shorter than me.

"Doesn't Mommy look beautiful?" Jolie says. "Like a princess."

"Oh, Jolie, Jax doesn't like princesses." Frankie smiles at me.

"Who doesn't like princesses?" Jolie asks.

Frankie shrugs. "Are we ready? We better get going since we have to take the train into the city."

"Let's go."

Once they both have their jackets on, I open up the door and Frankie tells Gumdrop that Grandma Sandy will be coming to let him out in a little bit. As if that will prevent him from pissing everywhere while she's gone.

We take the elevator down and file out of her apartment building to where our Uber sits waiting. No way we're taking the train dressed as if we're going to the opera.

"It's going to cost a fortune," Frankie says after Jolie's already crawled inside.

"It's my treat and stop thinking about money all the time."

We file in and the car ride takes about as long as the train ride, but Jolie's fascinated as we pass all the cities along the highway. As the buildings grow higher, her eyes grow bigger.

We arrive in Brooklyn and pull up in front of a church with guests outside, all in fancy dresses and suits. A big Catholic wedding indeed.

After the ceremony, Grandma Sandy is coming in to get Jolie and take her home while Frankie and I stay for the reception. What would we do without Grandma Sandy?

"There are so many people," Frankie says as we walk up the stairs.

Jolie comes between us, taking each of our hands. I'm not immune to the lingering stares at us. We walk in and grab programs, then we find Evan, Kamea, and Adrian in a pew toward the back, so we join them.

"Big wedding is an understatement," I say to Adrian.

"This is half the size Sierra's and mine will be if we get married in Sandsal. Which is why I fully intend on eloping." He laughs.

"If I ever got married, it might be the courthouse for me," I say.

Kamea rolls her eyes. "I thought you were never getting married?"

"And why the courthouse?" Evan asks.

"Because I don't care about the wedding. If I wanted to spend my life with someone, I sure as hell wouldn't need a bunch of people there to witness."

"Always going against the grain." Kamea looks over at Frankie. "I love your dress."

"Thanks," she says. "Yours too."

"That's the youngest brother," Evan says, pointing at a guy walking up the aisle after escorting someone down. "He's the real estate broker."

As if the guy knows they're talking about him, he winks. I've only met Blanca's brothers twice. They're cool guys, though they weren't what I was expecting when I heard they were loaded.

Carm—if I remember correctly—stops and puts out his hand to me. "Hey, Jax." After I shake his hand, he moves on to Adrian. "How's the prince?"

"Ah, not for much longer," Adrian says.

"Ladies." He winks again and leaves as Evan sighs.

"I'm going to tell Seth you're crushing on Blanca's brothers," I say down the pew.

Then a tall thin woman comes up to Carm and he embraces her, his hand squeezing her ass.

"That's his wife," Adrian tells her.

"Of course. She's gorgeous," Evan says.

Which she is, but she's not really my type.

"When is it going to start?" Jolie asks, getting down from the pew and lowering the foot riser.

"No, Jolie." Frankie leans forward and puts her hand on Jolie's arm.

But Jolie continues to do it. Other than the fact she's crushing my foot, I don't really see the harm in it.

What feels like a lifetime later, the music begins, and Ethan, Dylan, Knox, Seth, and Blanca's brothers all stand at the front.

"That's the oldest brother, then the middle one on the end," Evan tells Kamea as if she's in charge of the Mancini family tree.

The doors open, and Jolie gets up on her knees on the pew to get a better view. In walks who I believe is Dom's wife, Val, holding hands with a little girl as she tosses flowers. The girl is going so slowly, we're going to be here a long time. Dom walks to the front of the row to get her attention, but the girl doesn't care. Eventually Val picks her up and tosses the rose petals before handing the little girl to Dom.

Next comes Carm's wife, then Enzo's wife, who is pregnant. And then two other women I don't know, followed by

Rian then Sierra. After the bridal party is up front, the music changes, the doors open, and in walks Blanca with her dad.

"Oohs" and "aahs" ring out through the church. She smiles, and I look at Ethan. I don't know him nearly as well as the other guys, but his smile says he's happy as shit. All the stress I've seen them go through during this entire planning process of a big wedding, and it all comes down to this moment.

Blanca stares at Ethan through her veil, and the closer she comes to him, the more fidgety he becomes.

"They're so cute," Frankie whispers.

When Blanca reaches the end of the aisle, her dad raises her veil, kisses her cheek, and Ethan takes her hand. We all sit down, and the priest begins the ceremony.

What none of us were prepared for was the mass that comes before the wedding, and Jolie grows more and more impatient the longer it goes on. The riser is up and down, and she pokes the lady in front of us, which seems to mortify Frankie.

"I'm going to take her out," Frankie whispers.

But I hold Frankie's hand to keep her in place. She's probably enjoying this a lot more than me anyway.

"Let's go, Jolie," I whisper, take her hand, and walk her out of the church.

"Is it over?" she asks.

"No, but you're being disruptive, so we're going to chill out here until it's done."

"Weddings are boring." Jolie jumps down the hallway and I let her do it. She needs to burn off some energy.

A minute later, Dom comes out of the side entrance holding his daughter. He lowers her to the floor, and she walks over to Jolie, who introduces herself.

"Hey, Jax, right?" he says, shaking my hand.

"Hey, how are things?"

He shrugs. "Busy. I always wondered how a kid would affect my work life."

From the little I've heard Blanca talk about her brothers, Dom is by far the biggest workaholic out of all of them.

"Yeah, and?"

"It's more the whole family thing. First, we went through the whole crying thing at night and I never got any sleep. And then she was teething, then she was scared and had to sleep with us. Great for the sex life. Now she's finally sleeping in her own bed, but we can't go out to dinner or anywhere else because she's too fussy to sit still. Hence why I'm out here with you." He chuckles. He must notice Jolie for the first time. "Is she yours?"

"Nah, just a friend's."

"I was going to say, it got you too, huh?"

"It?" I ask.

"Cupid's arrow. For me, it wasn't really a surprise. I've loved Val almost my entire life, I just thought that…" He shakes his head. "Today's about love, right?" He squeezes my shoulder. "It takes some of us a while to get our heads out of our asses."

You're telling me this guy didn't have his shit together at some point? The man comes from a great family, has two parents who love him and a million other relatives. Mr. Holder is trying to find one relative to tell me if cancer runs in my family. My insecurities are justified; his aren't.

"I just didn't want to want for anything, and I felt like working my ass off was the answer. Turns out once I had all the money, I wanted a family to share it with. And that's a lot harder to get than money, let me tell you."

I nod, not interested in talking about this. Everyone comes out of foster care with a different view of life. I've never yearned for a family like Dylan did. I wanted safety, independence, and my freedom. Which I have. So why don't I feel totally fulfilled?

The doors open and Blanca and Ethan walk out, not even noticing Dom and me. They walk over to another room, and at the door, Ethan places his hands on her cheeks and kisses her like he probably wanted to in there. I watch like a peeping tom, sharing a moment that's none of my business. But their happiness is alluring, and it makes me think that maybe nothing could ever come between them.

As everyone files out, I snag Jolie from getting trampled and Dom grabs his daughter. Val comes by, and she and Dom laugh about once again being unable to enjoy something together since he had to take their daughter out.

"You remember Jax?" Dom says to his wife.

She leans forward, shaking my hand. "I guess they kept each other busy, huh?" She smiles at Jolie. Then they get pulled away by family members.

Frankie comes over. "Thanks."

"No problem."

"I'm going to call Sandy and see where she's at. I might have to walk Jolie down to the train."

"Come on, I'll go with you." I'm not interested in sticking around here. I'd rather make sure Jolie gets on the train safely with Sandy.

"Are you sure?" Frankie asks. "I can meet you later."

I place my hand on the small of her back. "I'm positive."

We leave the church, Jolie blowing the bubbles that would've been blown had we waited for Blanca and Ethan to leave the church. Frankie shivers next to me since she has a thin dress jacket on, so I shrug off my jacket and put it over her shoulders.

"Jax," she says.

I shake my head. "Let me do this one chivalrous thing," I say, and she lets it go.

We reach the train, and Sandy is already there, waiting to get Jolie.

"We'll let Gumdrop out, then sleepover at Grandma's," Sandy says to Jolie, who is bouncing with excitement. "You'll make sure she gets home safely?" Sandy asks me.

This is the first time I've wondered if it's weird for Sandy to see Frankie and me together. I mean, we're not a couple, or even on a date, but her son was with Frankie. They have a child together. Does Sandy hold any bitterness toward the fact that Frankie isn't with him anymore?

I nod. "She's safe with me."

She smiles, and we hug Jolie goodbye.

"Let's go to the reception," Frankie says.

"We have at least an hour. Do you think you can handle a drink before an open bar? I don't want to have to strip you down and shower you again."

Her finger pokes my ribs. "Stop it."

"I warned you. Try to tickle me and you'll be feeling my scruff between your thighs."

She says nothing, but her cheeks practically glow red.

And now I'm getting a hard-on. Jesus, why do I do this to myself?

CHAPTER EIGHTEEN

Frankie

*A*fter stopping for a drink at a bar, we arrive at the reception a tad late. Most everyone is already seated at their designated tables, so I grab our names and we head to the table with Evan, Kamea, Adrian, and a few of Blanca's high school friends.

We eat our meal amid polite conversation, and after we're done, the group disperses as if we were all chained there.

"I'm going to the restroom," I say before ducking out of the large ballroom and into the hallway.

In the bathroom, I pretend to put on my lipstick when really, I'm giving myself a mental pep talk. Every nerve in my body is magnetically surging toward Jax and I need to get these hormones under control before I embarrass myself and throw myself at him. After I've centered myself, I walk back to the ballroom. Not finding Jax anywhere, I head to the bar and get myself a club soda with lime. I'm playing it safe tonight. Throwing up on the train would top that night at Jax's.

Leaving the bartender a tip, I look across the room to try to spot someone I know. That's when I see Jax laughing with some girl. Okay, jealousy should not stab me with the force of a thousand knives—he's not mine—but it does anyway. All we have is a budding friendship. He thinks of commitment like a double life sentence.

Evan comes up to my side. "Who is that?"

"I don't know," I say.

"Jeez, could she touch more?"

Kamea joins us. "I think she works here. She's wearing the same outfit as the waitstaff."

So he's going to pick up some random chick who works here when we're supposed to go home together? Not that I can't get myself home. I can, and I don't need any help from him.

"Oh wait," Evan says and points. "Knox knows her."

Sure enough, Knox goes up to her and hugs her, smiling.

Kamea doesn't move. She's just as transfixed as I am. Though she has reason to be. Knox is her boyfriend. Jax is my... nothing.

The three of them talk like long-lost friends until another waitress tugs on her sleeve and she waves goodbye, disappearing through the kitchen doors. Knox and Jax talk for a moment until they look around, so the girls and I all huddle as if we weren't just gawking at them.

"Hey, ladies," Knox says, putting his arm around Kamea's waist and kissing her neck.

"Hey." She's sweet, not an ounce of jealousy in her tone.

Kudos to her.

"I was going to get you a drink," Jax says, nodding at the glass in my hand.

I raise it. "Got one."

"I see that." He narrows his eyes at me.

"What?"

"You okay?" he asks, tilting his head.

I nod, probably a little too much to pull off it being nothing. "Yeah, I'm great. It's a beautiful night."

Evan laughs because I'm totally laying it on too thick and need to pull it back a notch.

The night continues, Blanca and Ethan have their first dance, he dances with his mom, she dances with her dad, and they cut the cake. They throw the garter and the bouquet, which thankfully neither Jax nor I catch. I'm pretty sure neither of us was really trying though.

A slow song plays, and to my surprise, Jax holds out his hand. "Want to dance?"

"You dance?" I ask, surprised.

"Yes, I dance." He doesn't allow me to answer but takes my hand and guides me onto the dance floor.

Jax takes me in his arms, his fingers sliding under the strings that tie at the back of my dress. My skin heats and my nipples pebble under the silk of my dress. Being surrounded by his heat, in his arms, the feel of his breath on the side of my face—all it does is ratchet up the need I'm already feeling for him.

"This is probably a horrible idea," he murmurs.

"We don't have to dance."

He circles us around the floor. "I want to. That's the problem. Hell, if you would've caught the bouquet, I probably would've fought every guy for that garter belt just to put it on you with my teeth."

His willingness to tell me his every thought takes me aback.

"Did you take some sort of truth serum?" I ask.

He draws back so he can see my face. "No."

We continue dancing, and I notice the woman from

earlier that he was talking to is watching us from one of the side doors. She doesn't even try to turn away when she sees me notice her.

"Who is that woman?" I ask.

He turns us to see and sighs. "That's Naomi."

"Okay?"

"She's a girl we knew in high school." He glances around as though he wants to make sure no one will overhear him. "She was Dylan's girlfriend back then, and I slept with her."

"What?" I've always known Jax doesn't do the straight and narrow, but I've never known him to be as horrible as that.

"Not my proudest moment for sure. Dylan and I made amends when I returned. She was always playing us against one another. It's stupid really."

I glance back at her and see that she's still watching us with avid interest. "Well, I think she wants another few rounds with you."

He nods. "I know she does. That's why she thinks you're my girlfriend."

A stabbing sensation assaults my heart. "Is that why we're dancing?"

"Not at all." He turns me so that we get lost in a sea of people. "We're dancing because I want to be near you. I couldn't give a shit what she thinks."

"I'm so confused about what you want," I say, unwinding myself from his hold. Jax is the king of mixed signals lately.

He runs a hand through his hair. "I want you, Frankie, but I shouldn't." He looks as if it pains him to say the words.

"I can't keep playing this back and forth between us." I walk off the dance floor.

He grabs my wrist, pulling me back, circling us around. "I've never wanted a woman as much as I want you. But I'm not any good at this. I don't do relationships. I've been trying to keep my distance, but I show up at your apartment and you look like you do right now... how can I possibly keep myself from wanting you?"

"So what, I shouldn't dress up?"

He leans in, his lips falling to my collarbone. "God, no. You're gorgeous, stunningly beautiful. I want to undress you right here."

"Jax," I sigh, not sure what to say to that.

"Tell me I'm wrong. That you don't want me too?"

"I do."

"Then let's go."

He tugs on my hand, and we leave the reception without saying any goodbyes. We file into an Uber after he calls one, and the ride home is pure torture.

I should ask him what's going to happen after tonight, but part of me doesn't want to know. I know that makes me weak, but I've taken so many for the team. I want this one thing for myself. One sober night with Jax to allow him to show me how I should be treated.

His hand lifts my dress in the darkness of the back seat, his fingers grazing along the outside of my panties. I hold his wrist to stop him from going any further because I want to cherish every orgasm. I want to scream and moan and not have to bite my lip to be quiet when I come on his hand.

When we reach my apartment, Jax takes the keys from me. On the elevator, he corners me, the back of his hand sliding down over my nipples and they pebble immediately. His lips land on my collarbone again, traveling around to my neck as his hand molds to my hip. He turns me around, and his lips land on the back of my neck.

The elevator dings at my floor all too soon, and he whispers, "That's one."

We walk down to my apartment and he lets us in. Flipping the locks on the door, we see a note from Sandy.

Jolie wanted to bring Gumdrop, so I've got them both.

I've never wanted to kiss Sandy more in my life. If one of us had to let the dog out right now, I might've screamed.

"I'm going to sit in that chair and you're going to take off your dress for me. I want to see the moon illuminate your body." He unzips my side zipper to make it easier, then he sits in the chair, his hand gripping his cock through his dress pants.

I've never been more aroused in my life. My panties are soaked through by now and my insides clench as I lower one strap then the other, allowing the top of my dress to fall to my waist, exposing my bare breasts.

He groans, his hand continuing to grip his dick through his pants. "Turn around and slide it over your ass," he says in a rough voice.

I do as he instructs and shimmy the dress down. It falls to the floor after it clears the round globes of my ass. He groans again, and this time it's so deep, it's more of a growl. My hands move to the sides of my panties.

"I'll take care of those. Come here," he whispers as if someone else in my apartment might hear us.

The sound of a zipper fills the small room, and when I turn around to walk toward him, I see his pants are open and his cock is out. He opens his legs wider and my hands twitch, wanting to touch his hard length, to feel the weight of him in my palm. He leans forward, his fingers hooking on to the sides of my panties, and he slides them down my legs. His palms run up my calves to my thighs to my ass before he thrusts me forward and I lose my balance and straddle him.

"You shaved for me?" His hands continue to run over my legs, diving between my thighs. "You even trimmed for me, huh?"

"Who says it was for you? I just wanted to feel pretty," I lie.

He chuckles, taking my nipple into his mouth. I gasp at the sensation as he twirls his tongue around my hardened nipple before he sucks almost my entire tit into his mouth. He moves to the other side and repeats the same delicious torture. My fingers grip his hair, not wanting him to stop.

He rests his chin on my chest. "That's two."

I unbutton his shirt, needing to feel his skin on mine. He puts his hands on the side of the chair as though he prefers to torture himself and not touch me while I undress him. After I splay his shirt open to see his ink that is so perfectly placed with the thoughtfulness only an artist would have, my hand travels down his abs until I wrap it around his hard cock. He bucks into my hand and I smirk.

"I guess I have to do some finding myself, huh? Unless you want to tell me your three erogenous zones?" I kiss him, practically melting into him.

One of his hands lands on the back of my head, his fingers threading through my hair. He deepens the kiss and I shudder. His tongue is amazing, sending pulsing waves of pleasure right between my legs.

"You're on one right now." He bucks his hips up.

I'm not sure I have the willpower to continue this slow exploration when I really want him to pick me up and take me against the wall. "Hmmm, what else could there be?"

I pull back and his lips travel the length of my neck, his hands on the back of my head putting me in the position he wants me in. I crawl off his lap and fall to my knees in front of him. He shrugs off his shirt and I pull off his boxers and slacks, disposing of them with my dress on the floor. Then I take off each sock. Soon we're both naked except for the heels I still have on.

I run my hands up his legs, placing a feather-light touch

behind his knees and getting no reaction. I take hold of his cock and place the tip at my mouth.

He moves my hair out of my face to see me. "That's two."

I lick his length from base to tip, the whole time maintaining eye contact with him. "It's not the same one?"

"Different feel. Hand first. Mouth second." I shake my head at his absurdity, but he leans forward and picks me up from under my arms. "Want me to show you the third?"

I straddle his waist as he walks us back to my bedroom. "I can think of two other holes your dick can go into, and I hate to break it to you, I'm not game for one of them."

He chuckles and drops me on the bed. "I guess you'll find out." He winks. "But first I have to finish with your erogenous zones."

His face disappears between my thighs. That's when I learn that Jax's fingers aren't his only talented part—so is his mouth.

CHAPTER NINETEEN

Jax

I don't think I could ever tire of Frankie's taste. Her fingers grip the back of my head as I lick her pussy, concentrating on her nub. Knowing that I have to tease her, I draw away from and nibble on her inner thighs, running my tongue over the soft skin and allowing my scruff to cause friction. She attempts to close her legs as if it's all too much, but I slide my hands up her thighs and force her to spread herself for me.

"Jax," she sighs.

I say nothing as I flick my tongue on her swollen nub then retract, driving her crazy as her pelvis rises off the bed and chases my tongue.

"Please," she begs.

I go back and concentrate on her other thigh, circling my tongue. I push a finger inside her and she bolts up, her eyes drowning with ecstasy. Using two fingers now, I slowly glide them in and out while staring up at her and massaging her clit with my tongue. She's so hot when she's this close to coming. I can read her expressions and her moans, and I know she needs one more finger before she flies off into ecstasy.

When I add a third finger, her eyes widen and her hand clamps down on my wrist, her legs tightening around my head. She cries out, then she's there. I watch as she comes apart on my fingers.

"That's three," I murmur.

She falls back to the mattress and her legs widen after her orgasm has sucked away any energy she had. I lick her taste off my fingers while getting on my knees and positioning her hips for her pussy to meet the tip of my dick. She intently watches my fingers move in and out of my mouth, and by the time I thrust inside her, she's more than ready to coat my cock with her arousal.

"Oh God," she cries out, her hands falling to her tits and squeezing them. "That feels so good. Too good."

I'm not gonna lie, I've had my share of women in my bed. But Frankie, watching her unravel for me could be addicting —a high I would chase relentlessly because lately I feel as if there's a part of me who was put on this earth to make her happy. And she's clearly happy when I'm inside her.

"Jax. I can't. Not again." Her head whips side to side, her dark hair splaying across the mattress.

"You can, baby, just relax and enjoy."

I grip her hips and tug her closer, my balls slapping against her ass. I was a shameless bastard taking her from behind the first time. Scared that if I took her face-to-face, I'd feel just like I do right now. As if we're two puzzle pieces that might fit together. But the problem is she's all smooth edges and mine are jagged and sharp and I'm bound to cause damage if I try to push us together.

Her body twists and turns, rises and falls on the mattress as she takes the pleasure I'm forcing on her. She rises off the bed, bending forward. I lean toward her, allowing our lips to touch for a second before she falls back to the mattress, my name on her lips as her insides pulse against my straining cock.

"Jaxxxx."

I bend her legs forward once she's recovered. "Now it's time for my third erogenous zone."

A look of fear crosses her face and I chuckle, unable to go through with my joke. I position one of her smooth-as-silk legs to rest on my chest and the other straight out to her side. I pull my dick completely out of her pussy and push in to the hilt. She sighs as though she could come a third time.

Drilling in and out of her, I unapologetically take what I want. Frankie seems to get more turned on the rougher I am. I chase my orgasm, trying to push all of my feelings out of the equation, but I can't deny that when her fingers run down my chest, the perfect scrape of her nails makes me lose my battle, pumping into her before I still and spill into her.

Once I've come down from my orgasm, panic sets in. "Shit, we didn't use protection."

She smiles. "I have an IUD, no worries as long as you're clean."

Thank God. Where the fuck was my head? "After your sex bet with me, I haven't been with anyone but you since my last test."

"That makes two of us," she says.

I lie down next to her and our breathing normalizes. She's so close but so far away. I've never wanted to be close to a woman after I've had sex with them. Usually I'm already getting dressed after I dispose of the condom, so this feeling is new, and I can't decide if it's unwanted or not.

She rolls over and throws her arm over my chest. "I'm starving. Pizza?"

Yeah, we're gonna go with this tonight. "You read my mind." She giggles and shifts to climb off the bed, but I roll over, caging her to the mattress. "Allow me."

I kiss her, and she opens her thighs so my hips fall between them. I could definitely make this my new home. But I kiss her one more time and get off the bed in search of pizza.

———

THE PIZZA BOX sits in the middle of her living room, the television showing a repeat of *Friends*. I bend forward, my hand falling to her cheek, and I kiss her, sliding my tongue into her mouth.

She smiles when I close the kiss. "What was that for?"

I shrug. "I just wanted to kiss you."

My truthfulness seems to make her smile grow. Her head falls to the side and she examines me. Oh shit, she's going to ask me something I can't answer, or don't want to answer.

"I need to ask you a question." The tentative vibe in her voice says I should have kept my lips off hers.

"Yeah?" I wipe my hands and sip some of my water.

"What are we doing?"

I blow out a breath. I'm not prepared for this conversation, although I should've been before I slept with her a second time. The first time could be chalked up to us drinking and needing an escape after being at the lawyer's office that day. What happened tonight cannot.

"I'm not sure," I answer.

She nods and turns her attention back to the television.

I place my finger under her chin and bring her eyes to

face mine again. "That's not to say this is nothing... I'm just worried it could end horribly."

"Why do you think you can't be in a relationship? Honestly. Have you ever honestly tried?"

I open my mouth to give her my typical answer. I didn't grow up seeing examples of successful marriages. I saw fighting, fists flying, verbal and physical abuse.

But before I can speak, she continues, "I'm not looking for a wedding ring. I have a little girl to consider and her heart is already in her hands, waiting for you to accept it. The worst thing I could do as a mother is involve myself with someone who doesn't want to accept her. But you told me on that dance floor tonight that you felt it." Her finger moves between us. "This new energy between us. Don't you want to see where it could go?"

She's so strong and brave to open herself up like this and show me her vulnerability.

"You'll probably want to break up with me tomorrow morning," I say.

She nods. "Probably."

"I'm bound to ruin this."

"Definitely." She's smiling. "I'm not the type of woman who's going to beg you, Jax. Don't get me wrong, this is amazing. I wouldn't mind getting fucked by you on the regular, but booty calls and casual sex went out the window when she was born." She pats my knee. "All I ask is that if you can't give your full energy to this, then let's leave it be after tonight."

She stands, and I watch her walk into the kitchen. I sit there for a moment, the annoying laugh track on *Friends* making me feel as though they're laughing at me for thinking I could even entertain a real relationship. Then I think of Jolie. Frankie's right—it's not just about us. If things don't work out, I know myself well enough to know I'll flee, which means I'm leaving behind a little girl who would think she did something wrong. But at the same time, being with Frankie makes me feel like a better person. Like maybe there's more potential inside me than I think.

I push off the floor and walk into the kitchen. She's pulled a carton of ice cream from the freezer and the first spoonful is resting at her lips. I take the carton and spoon from her and place them on the counter. I press my hands on either side of her cheeks and seal my lips on hers. She wraps her arms around my neck, and I place my hands on her hips, hoisting her up onto the counter.

"You thought we bickered before? You're gonna get annoyed with telling me what to do," I murmur into her neck, licking my way up her earlobe.

"I'm pretty sure I'll be happy with the make-up sex."

I draw back and pretend I'm going to leave her a wanting mess on the counter, but she locks her ankles around my waist and laughs.

"We'll figure it out together," she says, resting her forehead against mine. "I'm no expert either."

My hands slide up the hem of her T-shirt and she sheds it, so I suck her tit into my mouth. I guess there are pluses to being in a relationship—mainly the fact I won't have to pretend not to want her every minute of the day.

"Jax," she moans, her fingers sliding through my hair as my hand grazes down her torso and slips under the waistband of her pajama pants, finding her slick and wet.

Yeah, I am definitely seeing some plus sides to us trying this dating thing.

She pulls back for a moment and I'm the one groaning. "I don't think we should tell Jolie right away. No sleepovers and no public displays of affection until we're really sure this is going somewhere."

I nod. I'm all for protecting Jolie.

"Please don't take that as me not trusting you."

I shake my head. "I wouldn't bet on me either, Frankie."

I descend on her tits again, but she takes my head in both her hands and pries me off. "I am betting on you, Jax. My heart is fragile too, but I'm a grown adult and own my decisions. Jolie would be the collateral damage here. Me not wanting to tell her has nothing to do with me not believing in you."

Jesus, where is the woman who hates me? The one who would roll her eyes at me and look at me as though I'd never grow up? Now she thinks I'm the one to bring her a happily ever after? She's crazy, but damn if she's not enough for me to want to try.

I pick her up off the counter, heading to the kitchen table so I have better access, but the buzzer rings. We stop and look at one another with frustration. Who the hell is cock-blocking me at this time of night?

She flies off the table, pressing the button. "Hello?"

"Frankie," a man's voice says. "Let me up."

She looks at me with wide eyes. I've never seen her scared like this. "Who is it?"

"Michael."

I press the button to let him up. Time for Michael and me to have a conversation. But first I need to put on pants.

CHAPTER TWENTY

Frankie

"What are you doing?" I ask Jax as he walks across the room and puts on his dress pants from earlier.

He buttons his pants and looks at me. "You need to put something on."

I look down and head into the kitchen to pull my shirt over my head. "I'm serious. It isn't your job to fix this."

"I'm going to pretend that we didn't just agree to be something more to each other seconds ago and argue that I'm your friend too."

Anxiety eats away at my insides. "This is a really bad idea."

Michael knocks on the door. It's the middle of the night, which means he's probably drunk or high—or both. The only good thing about this is that Jolie isn't here to witness whatever is about to go down.

Jax walks to the door with his shoulders straight as though he's ready to start a fight. I run and block his path, throwing myself between him and the door. Tonight was going so well. "Promise me you won't lose your temper."

His face softens for a minute and he leans in and places a chaste kiss on my forehead. "I'm not gonna do anything of the sort." His hand goes for the doorknob.

Some of the anxiety leaves my body.

When Jax opens the door, Michael leans back and checks the number of the apartment, probably thinking he's standing at the wrong one. "Who the hell are you?"

"Jax," he answers.

I peek my head around Jax. "It's not a good time, Michael."

"Come on in for a second. We need to have a chat." Jax steps aside, and I step back.

Michael steps into the apartment. "Who are you? Her boyfriend?"

I shouldn't be waiting on Jax's answer as eagerly as Michael is.

"Yes," Jax responds with confidence.

"Well, that's great, but what I'm here for has nothing to do with you. Where's Jolie?" His pupils are little dots, a clear sign he's been using, and not just alcohol tonight.

"She's not here," I say.

He walks around the living room. "Why? So you could have your boy toy over? How convenient. And you say you want sole custody of her?"

"Just leave," I say.

He pulls papers out of his jacket. Man, Mr. Holder found him fast as soon as he came back into town. "Give me one reason I should sign this?"

"Because you can't care for her. I told you, if you get

clean, I'm more than willing to reevaluate, but you're not someone who should be in her life right now."

He slams his fist on the wall. "I'm her father!"

Jax steps forward, but I slide between him and Michael. This is my problem. Not Jax's.

"I'm not going to have this conversation again," I say. "You're not good for her right now. All you bring her is heartbreak. If you want to get sober, go to rehab and we'll talk."

He looks at me, then behind me to where I can feel Jax's breath on my neck. "I'm just supposed to let this guy slide into my spot in this family?"

I shake my head. "We're not a family. You know that."

Whatever drug he's on right now, he's allowing me to talk to him and there's no anger blaring from his eyes. It's a welcome change.

I ask, "What if you hit her? You already hit me when you were using. I know you're not normally violent, but you're not you when you're messed up."

He squeezes his eyes shut. "I said I was sorry."

"I know you are, but if you don't get help, there's no way I can allow you to spend time with her. And I know the man I first met, the one who I hope is still in there, agrees. He'd never want his daughter to be hurt the way he was."

Michael collapses on the couch. "But if I sign this, then it's over. The court will never let me be in her life."

"I'm her mother. I have a say too." I hate lying to him, because although I wish Michael would get clean, the chances are slim at best. He has to do the work. I can't do it for him. All I can do is protect myself and my daughter. And although Jax is ready to step in, *I* have to handle this. "Please think about what's best for her. Sign the papers, get yourself clean, and then we'll talk."

He looks at the papers and back up at me. His eyes seem

sincere as he nods, but right as I step forward, he shakes his head. When he looks at me again, I see someone else there.

"I'm not going to sign anything and let this douchebag be her father. She's mine!" Michael rips apart the papers and they sprinkle to the floor. "Fucking hell, Frankie, how could you do this to me?"

"Me?" I point at myself. "I'm not the one who just showed up high and a hot mess."

"All you are is a fucking bitch! A whore who spreads her legs for anyone!" He nods at Jax.

Jax walks around me and nudges me behind him. "I'm going to tell you this once—you are not welcome to show up on Frankie's doorstep unannounced. And you don't speak to the mother of your child like that. She's the one raising your daughter, working her ass off because you can't man up and take care of your responsibilities."

Michael cocks his fist back, but Jax punches him before Michael gets the chance. He stumbles, but Jax grabs Michael's shirt to keep him upright, his fist at the ready again.

"You think you're some tough guy, hitting a woman?" Jax hits him again.

I grab Jax's arm to stop him and he lowers his arm to his side, letting Michael go.

Michael stumbles back and loses his footing, falling to his ass. "Fuck you, asshole."

"Get the hell out of here! And I meant what I said—don't show up here again without contacting Frankie first to make sure it's okay," Jax yells.

Michael stands and holds his eye that's already swelling. "Nice people you hang out with, Frankie, I'm sure my lawyer would like to hear about this guy." He looks Jax up and down as though he's not intimidated.

Jax glares at him, waiting for Michael to make a move so he can put him on his ass again.

"Just leave," I say, fighting back tears.

Michael huffs. "Figures you'd fall for a guy like this. You always did like the damaged guys, right? That way you can hide all your scars underneath theirs. Good luck with her," he says to Jax. "She'll make you think you're the screwed up one, but really it's her."

Jax steps closer so they're chest to chest. "Do you need me to show you the door?"

Michael laughs, continuing to hold his face. "See you in court."

He walks out, and Jax locks the door. I sit on the couch and rock back and forth, clenching my shaking hands.

Jax comes to the floor in front of me, taking my hands. "He's an asshole. Don't listen to him. He's high and probably doesn't even know what he's saying."

"I just want him out of my life, but he's Jolie's father, so he'll always be part of it."

Jax sits next to me, sliding me onto his lap. "I think it's time you leave this apartment. I don't like the idea of him showing up at night when you're here by yourself."

"I'm fine."

"Does he come by a lot in the middle of the night?" Jax asks.

I could lie, but that's not exactly the best start to a relationship. "Sometimes. Not lately, because he left town, but something obviously brought him back. I'll have to call Mr. Holder in the morning."

We sit in the chair, *Friends* playing in the background, the two of us lost in our own thoughts.

"Move in with me," Jax says.

My head whips in his direction. "No."

"I'm not gonna take no for an answer. You're not safe

here. Neither is Jolie. He never comes around Ink Envy and he wouldn't even know about the Rooftop Apartments, so you're safe there. If he wants to see Jolie and you're agreeable, you can meet somewhere else. Or if you want to tell him where you're living, at least everyone else is there in case he shows up unexpectedly."

I climb off his lap. "I'm fine. We're good here." I pace across the room, looking out the window at the quiet winter night.

"Please don't," he says so softly I barely hear him.

"Don't what?" I turn and press my back to the window.

"Don't push me away." There's so much emotion in his voice, I can't speak past the lump in my throat. "You know on game night when you got sick?"

I bury my head in my hands. "Way to make the mood even more somber."

He chuckles. "I liked seeing that side of you."

"You liked seeing the side of me that had no control and threw up all over you and your couch?" He's crazy, what is he even saying?

"I liked seeing your vulnerable side. Don't get me wrong, I fucking love how strong you are. The way you are with Jolie and the way you take shit from no one, especially me. But I also liked that there was a side of you that needed me. And I liked being the one who got to take care of you."

"Jax—" I shake my head in disbelief.

He holds up his hand to stop me from speaking. "You're a badass, there's no arguing that. But this situation with Michael has to be scaring you. And if you really want to give this thing between us a shot, you have to let me in. Now I'm not saying that whatever Michael said was true, and I don't give a shit even if it is. If you want to trust me with any baggage you have, I'm here. But if we're going to work, you have to lean on me and let me help you sometimes. You have to let me in to see the sides of you that you guard the most."

His words are too much, and I sink to the floor and bury my head between my legs.

I hear Jax rise and cross the room. "We all have our shit. Hell, you know mine. But let me help you here. Move in with me. Not because of what's happening between us, but because I'm your friend first and foremost." He rubs his hand up and down my back.

"I can handle him."

He places his finger at my lips. "I know you could handle this on your own if you had to, but that's my point. You don't have to get through this alone."

I sniffle, trying to keep the tears inside.

In true Jax fashion, he tries to lighten the mood. "Please let me keep my balls here and act all apeshit protective over you and Jolie. Just give me this."

I chuckle and lose the fight and nod. "Separate bedrooms?"

He smiles. "Sure, but don't kick me in the balls in the middle of the night when I sneak in."

"And as soon as the Michael thing is over, we move out." I hold his gaze.

He nods. "Sure."

"I'm serious," I say.

"So am I. I don't want you there any longer than you have to be anyway." His smile says he's playing the part for me.

"Good. I'm just afraid you might get too attached to Jolie and me."

He laughs again and puts his arm around my shoulders. "I'm already attached."

"And I pay half the rent."

He shakes his head.

"I'm serious. There are two of us and one of you."

"Fine, you can pay the electric bill."

I elbow him in his stomach.

"And the gas."

"Jax, you have to let me pay."

He huffs. "Fine."

I lean on his shoulder, and he kisses the top of my head. "Thank you."

"It's nothing. What are friends for, right?"

His words warm my chest, but I'd be lying if I said I didn't wish he said boyfriend. I'm fully aware of the hard road ahead of us—because he's going to be constantly fighting with himself about whether he's boyfriend material—but I'm optimistic that he'll start to see himself like I do.

CHAPTER TWENTY-ONE

Jax

I had no idea a woman and a little girl could have so much stuff. Looking around my apartment, I see toys in one corner for Jolie, crap on all the tables, and a blanket over the couch.

Frankie comes out of her room. "Oh, hey, you're home."

I nod.

She laughs. "Want to take back your offer?"

"No, just remind me tonight after Jolie's in bed why I suggested this."

She shakes her head and crosses the room. "She's across the hall right now." Her finger dips into the waistband of my jeans.

"Then why are we dressed?" I press my lips to hers, backing her up to the counter.

It's only been two days since we had the talk about our relationship, and I haven't regretted it. In fact, I'm liking the sneaking around from Jolie a little too much. I think it's because it goes along with my love for breaking the rules.

Her hands slide over my shoulders, pushing my leather jacket until it slides down my arms and onto the floor. I cradle her face between my hands and tilt her head to deepen the kiss exactly how I like it, and she moans. Tonight is our first night in the same apartment with neither of us having somewhere else to go. Scary as that thought is, I'm swallowing my fear. Moments like this make me forget what we're doing.

The door opens and she pushes me off her. I circle around until my hands are splayed on the fridge.

"*Jax!*" Jolie jumps over to me.

I shift my weight to situate myself before I scare the poor girl.

But she doesn't run for me, thank God. She picks up my jacket. "Mommy doesn't like coats on the floor. She likes them on the coat rack." She hangs my coat on the lowest hook, and I look at Frankie, who's laughing. After she hangs up my jacket, Jolie takes my hand. "Come look at my room. Mommy spent all day making it nice."

I walk into her small room, which used to be Knox's. We gave Jolie this one since it's the farthest room from mine. That way when Frankie sneaks into my room, we're less likely to wake her.

Sure enough, you'd think Jolie picked up her room at their apartment and put it in here. Her rainbow nightlight is plugged into the wall, her bed is pushed against the same wall, and her bookcase is filled the way it was in her old room.

"Love it," I say.

Jolie hops on her bed, patting it for Gumdrop to join her, but he's not big enough yet to jump up there. I leave them to it and walk back into the living room to find Frankie dusting my lampshade.

"What are you doing?" I ask.

"Dusting."

Hmm…

I'm about to sit down and play my video game, turning off whatever this cartoon is, when Jolie runs out, grabs my hand, and tugs me. "Jax, we have to get Earl. Winston keeps peeing on him."

How is that tree not dead yet?

"But he likes Glenda," I say, not about to bring the tree over to our place to take up the little space we have left on our balcony. Let it stay on Dylan and Rian's massive one.

"Come on."

"Jolie, let Jax relax. He's not one of your toys," Frankie says.

I appreciate the effort, but Frankie's crazy if she thinks that's gonna work. I guess nights to myself are over now.

I let Jolie tug me into Dylan and Rian's apartment, where she declares, "We're here for Earl."

Dylan looks up from his magazine, a game playing on the TV. I'm already mourning my single life.

"Oh good, because Glenda has to go to the farm. She's about to cause a fire." He puts down his magazine and follows us to the balcony.

"A fire?" Jolie says.

I stand on the balcony, examining the trees. Earl has lost at least half its needles and those that are left are turning a nasty shade of brown. "You know what? I think we should let Earl escort Glenda to the farm, so she's not scared."

Jolie gives me the same look Frankie does when I say something that pisses her off.

"Or not." I raise my hands.

"Jolie, Glenda is really scared," Dylan says.

She rolls her eyes. I'm not sure even she can deny how sad both trees look. "Okay, but I'm not watching." She huffs and walks back into the apartment.

Dylan bends down, laughing, and pets Winston. "I think he's going to miss Earl more than Jolie will."

"Once more for old time's sake?" I ask Winston who plops down. "Okay, never mind. Let's go."

I pick up Earl, and Dylan picks up Glenda. We take them down the elevator to the trash, then place them next to the garbage container. It's freezing and I rush back inside.

As we wait at the elevator, it's clear Dylan wants to ask me something. We've known each other forever, so I know his tells by now. Dylan caught Frankie and me kissing when we were moving her out. Ever since, he's been giving me the silent treatment. I sigh and look at him.

"She's a kid, you know?" he says softly.

I knew he'd be the one to lecture me. "I know."

"This isn't something you can fuck up, Jax. She was hurt horribly for the first three years of her life. And Jolie asked Santa for you to be her daddy. Are you really sure about this?"

"We're not telling Jolie until we know what this is."

He blows out a breath. "There's still Frankie to consider. And do you think moving them in with you is going to make Jolie not want you to be her daddy more?"

The elevator comes, thank God.

"Listen, they had nowhere else to do." My hands fist when I think about how scared Frankie looked when Michael was in her apartment. "He showed up at her place at two in the morning. She said he does it a lot. I wasn't going to let them stay there and neither would you."

We step in, and he presses the button in the elevator like he's pressing mine right now. "They could stay with us, you know that. Are you serious about this whole relationship thing?"

"I like her."

"Liking her isn't good enough, not in this scenario. Your feelings need to be a helluva lot stronger than *like* to move them in with you."

We arrive at our floor and I file out first, eager to get away from Dylan and his lectures. We're both at our doors and I'm about to walk in when I decide I'm not going to let this go.

I spin around. "You know what? You're supposed to be my friend. Don't you believe in me? You seem pretty sure I'm gonna fuck this up."

He turns around. "I see two of my good friends, who haven't had the easiest road, trying something that has a less-than-good probability of working out. Remember when we were younger and as you got older, the chances of you being adopted shrunk more and more?"

I nod.

"I'm not even saying it's you, Jax. You could be the one who ends up hurt. You think she trusts easily? Add onto that the fact that you keep people at arm's length? I want you two to work, I think you're great for one another, but it *is* work. Relationships aren't just sex when you want it."

"You think I don't know that?" I scowl at him.

He shrugs. "Only time will tell. I do hope it works out, but there's a lot going against you." He opens his door and disappears inside his apartment.

Never in my life did I think Dylan would think so little of me.

I open the door to find that Frankie's still cleaning. Jolie's in the corner trying to get Gumdrop to drink out of a teacup. Cartoons are playing on the television. Maybe Dylan has a point. I'm the farthest thing from a dad you can get.

LATER THAT NIGHT, after Jolie goes to bed, Frankie's in my arms, in my bed. I'd like Dylan to see us now so I could give him the finger.

Frankie rests her chin on my stomach, her finger outlining the compass on my chest. The one I got with Dylan at sixteen. How stupid were we to get ones that were supposed to speak to the other? His was supposed to remind me to anchor down my wild streak, while my compass was supposed to push him to explore and take more chances in his life.

"What's it like being Instagram famous?" she asks.

I always felt Frankie despised me for my fandom on Instagram. That she took it as selling out. "I'm not famous."

"You have people flying from all over to see you. You could be making so much money if you left Ink Envy."

I shrug, not sure if I want to open up to her. But Dylan's opinion that we have to be vulnerable together or it will never work triggers me. Plus, I can't tell Frankie to let me in if I'm not going to do the same. "When I first left, I did it because Dylan and I had a falling out—over that Naomi chick. I enjoyed the bit of fame I got. I'd never experienced anything like it. People always wanting to hang with you. The money was so good I thought I was dreaming. But it's all fake. Everyone wants something from you, and if they don't get it, they just leave after a while. I still talked to Knox, and he heard it one night."

"Heard what?" she asks.

"Heard my sadness." I shrug again. "He told me to come home. That it was time."

She's quiet, staring at me. "Home sounded nice. I've never really had a home, but Knox told me about the setup here and how great everyone was. I'd wanted to make amends

169

with Dylan for years by that point, so I agreed. Thought I'd be here a few weeks, recharge, and leave, but Dylan needed me."

"To work at Ink Envy."

I nod. She knows firsthand how the business wasn't thriving when I first showed up. "Where we come from, you help each other out. And plus, Dylan is so talented, he could've been me and had the same success I'd had if he'd gotten out there."

She smiles and kisses my chest. "I think there's only one Jax Owens."

I run my hand down her tattooed back. "True, but you and Dylan are mad talented. I think it was just the circumstances that got me to where I was. If you didn't have Jolie, you could've gone down the same path as me. But there's something to be said for having loyal friends."

"That's for sure."

"I think when I was younger, I was hell-bent on getting out of the neighborhood, making something of myself, and I took my friendships for granted. I'll never make that mistake again."

She lays her head on my chest again. "My family disowned me."

I blink in surprise. "Why?"

"Because I didn't want to stay in Wisconsin. Because I wanted to go to school for art. Because I was a little wild and never really fit their mold. There're a lot of reasons. I ran away after high school." I pull her closer and she looks up at me. "Our relationship has always been strained. We rarely talk. They know nothing about Michael because I didn't want to hear 'I told you so' from them. They send Jolie birthday gifts and Christmas gifts, but that's it."

"I'm sorry."

She nods. "I have Sandy. I'm not sure what I would do

without her. But I always wanted to be a huge success and throw it in my parents' faces. To say I told you so, I told you I could make it."

"You're a great mom and so talented. You don't need a bunch of Instagram followers to prove that."

"It would be nice though. Not that I would choose not to have had Jolie. I mean, she's my reason for living right now. But maybe if I would have had a sliver of the fame."

I tuck a strand of her dark hair behind her ear, and she climbs on me. She's just as insatiable as I am.

"Come to Vegas with me?" I ask. "It's just a weekend. I'm sure we can find someone to watch Jolie. I'll arrange it so you have your own spot. Do the pop-up with me?"

Her forehead falls to my chest. "No way. I'm not good enough for that."

I cradle her head in my hands and tilt her so she's looking at me. "You are. I'd never suggest it if you weren't."

"Are you sure it's not just your dick talking?"

The fact she didn't deny me right off the bat says I'm getting somewhere with her. "Come."

She bites her lip, and just when I expect her to say no, she nods. "Okay."

I roll us over and kiss her because the fact that she'll do it even though I know she's scared says how strong she is. That turns me on just as much as her vulnerable side does.

Vegas, here we come.

CHAPTER TWENTY-TWO

Frankie

"*I*'m not sure I can go with you to Vegas," I tell Jax three days after I agreed to go with him. I think it was the post-orgasm bliss that had me agreeing in the first place.

"Why?" He spits toothpaste into the sink while I'm trying to pull back my hair.

"Not until the Michael thing is taken care of. I mean, what if he somehow…" I don't finish the thought. It's just not an option for me to be thousands of miles away from her with him still in Cliffton Heights. "I'm going to talk to Mr. Holder today." I poke my head out of the bathroom and check the clock on the DVR. "Crap, I gotta get going."

I move to leave, but Jax shuts the bathroom door. His hands slide up my torso and he casts a trail of open-mouth kisses along the back of my neck.

He pinches my nipples through my bralette and his

mouth travels to my ear. "I love it when your hair is up. You're going to torture me all day with your neck exposed like this."

I sink back into his strong chest. "It is one of my zones."

His lips trail across the back of my neck and he grows harder behind me. I'd love nothing more than to have him take me from behind right now. Bend me over this sink and take what we both want while we watch in the mirror. But a pounding sound on the door has me closing my eyes.

Jax positions my bralette back over my breasts and chuckles. "The warden has spoken."

"Mommy! Jax!"

I'm sure this is not what Jax signed up for. I straighten my ponytail and open the door with a smile.

"What are you doing?" Jolie asks, peering into the small space.

"Just showing Jax how to floss." I walk out.

Jolie doesn't look like she believes me. Jax holds up his floss as if I were telling the truth.

Liar, liar, pants on fire, that's what we are.

"I have to get to school." She's right behind me.

"I know, and I have an appointment." I look at her plate. "You didn't eat anything."

"The yogurt tasted funny," she says.

"And the waffle?"

"I'm over waffles. I don't want them anymore. Can we stop by Sweet Infusion and get a muffin?" Her eyes light up.

She's had so much change in her life recently, although I think she loves living here with everyone. Evan does crafts with her, Seth plays games with her, Rian bakes with her, and Dylan lets her talk nonstop. Blanca and Ethan are on their honeymoon. She skips from apartment to apartment way too freely for a five-year-old.

"I'll take her, you go." Jax steps out of the bathroom. He's had to resort to wearing basketball shorts instead of boxers around the apartment.

"Are you sure?" I ask.

Jolie jumps up and down. "Yay! You haven't seen my school yet."

"No, I haven't." He heads to his room. "Give me five minutes."

"Jax, are you sure?" I hate to put some sort of co-parenting vibe out there—I figure it's the quickest way to ruin our budding relationship—but I am late to Mr. Holder's.

"Positive. Go." He nods toward the door.

I give Jolie a huge hug. "See you after school." I tap her nose with my finger.

I leave the two of them to be self-sufficient while I run over to the lawyer's office before I'm so late that he won't see me.

MR. HOLDER IS the one who comes out to greet me. "Morning, my receptionist is sick."

"I'm sorry."

"I feared you might be too." He walks down the hallway to his office and shuts the door behind us. "Have a seat."

"Sorry about that, just running late."

"Children do that to you." He sits behind his big ornate desk and picks up a file folder that's thicker than it should be. "So you wanted to see me?"

"I want this over with. I'm done with being in limbo."

He looks at me and nods. "It's hard, I know, but I warned you it would be a long process, remember?"

Yeah, that's what put me in tears when I left here. "I just want it over. Tell me what to do."

"Well, we finally got the papers to him. We have a hearing

date, and if he doesn't show up, that will just extend the process further—but it will also be good for us."

"But—"

He holds up his hand. "I know. This has already gone on longer than you'd like. The best case scenario in this situation is that he signs the papers himself. That he decides on his own to give you sole custody. That's the fastest, most straightforward way, but rarely does that happen."

"He showed up at my apartment and tore up the paperwork. He has no intention of signing."

He leans back in his chair. "Is there anyone who might have some influence over him? Someone's opinion he'd value and who could point out the harm he's doing to Jolie? I know we've talked about addiction... I can change the paperwork to say that full custody remains only while he's using and that if he gets himself clean and offers drug tests that we'll amend the agreement. The problem right now is that you never filed a police report, and he has no arrest history, making it that much harder to prove him an unfit parent. Eventually we'll get there, but I'd hate for you to pay so much to get there, do you understand?"

I nod. That reminds me... "By the way, that check still hasn't cleared, so I wrote you a new one." I pull it out of my purse and slide it across his desk.

He accepts it. "I'll check with my accountant."

"Just cash this one."

"Okay." He puts it in his drawer.

I want to say if that's the way he's handling his finances, it's no wonder my check was never cashed, but I keep my thoughts to myself.

"So you think the fastest and easiest way about this is to get him to sign."

"It'll save you a lot of time and money." He hands me a file with the paperwork in it. "He has to sign with a notary."

"This is a tall order, Mr. Holder."

He chuckles. "I understand, but unless he gets arrested, it's essentially his word against yours."

I don't want Michael in jail. I just want him out of mine and my daughter's life. "Okay. Thank you."

He stands. "If all else fails, we still have our court date, and we'll get you sole custody that way. This is just the shorter road."

"Thanks."

"But listen, you're not to put yourself in harm's way to make this happen. That's not what I'm saying. Find someone else who might have some pull in his life."

I nod.

"Good, I'll walk you out."

I say goodbye to him and leave the office, the paperwork feeling heavy in my bag. How will I ever get Michael to sign these papers? I need this situation resolved, not just for the good of my daughter, but for the good of Jax's and my relationship. We've infiltrated his life and apartment more than he thought we would. If I have any hope of a future with him, I need to get my ass out of that apartment. Otherwise one day he's going to crack and wonder what he was thinking.

I head into work, the building dark since I'm the first to arrive. I flip on the lights and put my stuff away by my station, then go in the back and start the coffee maker. When I come back out, Sandy's there.

"Sandy?" I ask.

She offers me a nervous smile but doesn't move.

"What's going on?" I walk over to her and lead her to a chair in the waiting room. "Sandy? Are you okay?"

She blinks and grabs my hands, squeezing them. "I'm so stupid."

"What? What do you mean?" I ask.

"He came to visit me, said he wanted to get clean, that he was ready."

I nod slowly. "Okay."

"I let him stay the night." She looks at me as though I should know what happened next. "He stole all my jewelry. Luckily, I had my purse in the safe. But he took the baseball cards he and his dad saved all those years. They're probably worth nothing." She bends forward and cries. "I thought finally, finally he's seen what he's been doing. That he had a wake-up call, maybe when he found you and Jax." She shakes her head. "I almost told him where you guys were, but I said you haven't needed me lately, so I didn't know where you'd gone."

"Thank you," I say, relief washing through me.

She looks at me. "Have you spoken to the lawyer? He mentioned a court date last night. Wanted me to hire him a lawyer."

"And what did you say?"

"I said he had to go to rehab first."

I lean back in the chair. "The lawyer wants me to get him to sign papers in front of a notary. That it's the fastest way to get this all resolved."

Sandy's shoulders sink and she shakes her head. "He'll never do it."

"I know."

The door opens and Lyle barrels in. "Vegas, baby! You must be so excited. I just saw your name right next to Jax's on Instagram. Awesome." He takes out his Airbuds. "Hey, Sandy."

"What is he talking about?" Sandy asks.

I shake my head. "Nothing."

"Nothing?" Lyle can't seem to take a hint. "She's going to Vegas with Jax while he does a pop-up event. It's a huge deal.

Her name is gonna be out there and people will see her work. It's a great opportunity."

"Really?" Sandy smiles and grips my hands.

"I'm not going," I say to her and Lyle. "I can't."

"Why not?" Sandy asks. "I'll take Jolie. I never would've allowed him in if she was there. You know that, right?"

"I do." I nod. "I just can't leave. Not with everything up in the air. And there's no way Jolie can come with us."

"Oh, sweetie, you deserve it." She squeezes my hands.

"Jolie's first. Always."

The door opens again, and Jax walks in and pats Sandy on the shoulder. "Hey, Sandy. Lyle. Don't worry, she's safe in her chair in class. I walked her in."

"You walked her in?" I ask. "She let you?"

He puts his stuff on his chair and shrugs out of his jacket. "She said no, but I insisted."

I shake my head. "And?"

"I think the teacher thinks I'm her manny," he says. "I did ask Annabelle where she put her fourth-place trophy."

"You did not?" I ask, rolling my eyes.

"I told her Jolie's first place one is on her nightstand and she kisses it every night."

"Seriously?"

He chuckles. "No. I'm not a complete asshole. Especially to a kid." Then he must realize Sandy's been crying because he looks between us. "Everything good?"

I nod.

"No, Frankie said she's not going to Vegas," Sandy says.

He nods. "I know, but there will be another time. I'll make sure of it."

Sandy stands. "No, there won't."

"Yeah, there will. They're talking about doing something again in six months." Jax doesn't even realize what Sandy's saying.

She holds out her hand to me.

"What?" I ask.

"Give them to me."

I shake my head. "Sandy—"

She passes through the half door and marches over to my station. "No. You've sacrificed enough. I'm done sitting back. He's my son, I'll deal with him." She opens up my large purse and grabs the manila envelope.

"Sandy, it's fine. We'll get it handled eventually. My lawyer said that this is just a longer road."

"And what? We wait until he bankrupts you? No." She points at Jax. "Book her a ticket. She's on that plane."

He smiles and nods.

"I'll be back," she says.

"Sandy," I say, rushing over to her.

But she doesn't stop as she walks out of Ink Envy and right to her car, pulling away before I get the papers back.

Jax meets me at the door, his arms around my waist pulling me back to him. "I'll book a room with a Jacuzzi?"

I lightly elbow him in the stomach. "Cheesy."

"Such a dirty mind. I was simply thinking you'd be sore."

"Sore from what?"

"Putting your killer art all over people's bodies. Dirty girl," he whispers and kisses my neck.

We turn to head to our stations, and Lyle looks between us, waving his finger. "Are you two?"

"Yeah," Jax says and looks at me as though I'd have a problem with him declaring our relationship.

He couldn't be more wrong.

179

CHAPTER TWENTY-THREE

Jax

*F*rankie's still a mess as we board the airplane.

"Jolie's fine," I repeat for the hundredth time.

Sandy worked some sort of crazy magic. It took her a week, but she got Michael to sign the papers. He did make Holder write an amendment that stated that if he went to rehab and got clean, that the rights would be revisited. But Sandy also gave him money. She didn't say how much, but enough for him to leave town for some opportunity with a buddy.

I feel bad for Jolie. Although she knows none of it, one day she'll understand that her dad put using ahead of her.

"I've never left her, Jax," Frankie says, sliding into her seat.

She hasn't even noticed we're in first class. So far, this quick trip I thought would let me earn my membership in the mile high club isn't starting out how I planned.

"I know, but she's with Sandy, Dylan, and Rian. Everyone will watch her. They love her like she's their own."

She nods, and I flag down the flight attendant and ask for two shots.

Frankie shakes her head. "I don't think I'm drinking in front of you ever again."

"Don't be ridiculous." I hand her the glass the flight attendant poured the shot into.

She downs it and hands it back to me. "That's it though."

Pulling out her phone, she sends one last text to Rian, who has Jolie today. All I see are emojis as I lean over her shoulder to snoop. Rian responds immediately.

Rian: *Go have lots of loud sex with your boyfriend.*

"Smart girl," I whisper.

Frankie shakes her head, and the flight attendant comes over the speaker, asking us to put our phones on airplane mode.

Frankie holds her phone, but I take her hand, leaning back in the chair. "We're going to be back before you know it."

She says nothing but stares out the window.

Our flight is uneventful—which means I did not earn membership into the mile high club. I'm crossing my fingers it'll happen on the way back.

We get our luggage and I call for an Uber to take us to the hotel. Frankie calls home as soon as we're in the Uber, and Rian must hand the phone to Jolie because I hear her voice through the phone.

"Hey, sweetie," Frankie says, putting the call on speakerphone.

"Hi, Mommy. Guess what?"

"What?"

"Uncle Dylan walked me into school and the teacher asked if I had two daddies." She laughs as though she can't believe the teacher would think that.

"Oh, that's funny." Frankie gives me the side-eye for some reason.

"Then Annabelle told her I didn't have a daddy."

Seriously, can I kick a five-year-old's ass?

"Oh, baby," Frankie says.

"I told her that I'd rather only have a mommy than parents who fight like hers."

"Jolie!" Frankie scolds.

I laugh, and even the Uber driver stifles a laugh.

"That's what Jax told me. He said I should be happy for what I have."

I bite my lips as Frankie's head turns my way and she glares at me in a way I haven't seen in the past few weeks. I hold up my hands.

"Well, that wasn't a nice thing to say either," Frankie says.

"I'm making Valentines with Rian," Jolie carries on as if Frankie weren't trying to impart some wisdom.

I completely forgot Valentine's Day is coming up. I've never had a girlfriend for Valentine's Day. What will she expect? Jewelry? Roses? Hell, I have no idea.

"That's nice."

"We gotta go, Mommy. Love you!" The phone clicks off.

Frankie shoves it inside her purse. "Nice, Jax."

"The kid is an asshole just like her parents. I'm not apologizing."

Sometimes the nicer kid has to give it back to the bully to get them to back off. Frankie should know that.

We reach the hotel and I tip the Uber guy because he has a sense of humor. After we check-in, Frankie can't stop checking out the place as we walk to the elevator.

"Are you a first-timer?" I ask.

She nods. "Yeah."

I've been here so much, it could be my second home. "Well then, first we fuck, then I take you on a tour?"

"Really? I wanted to ask, but I didn't know if you'd be up for it."

I hate how part of her is scared to ask me to do things. As though I'm going to refuse anything that makes her happy. Goes to show you how much damage Michael did to her.

"What do you want to see?"

We step in the elevator.

"This is going to sound stupid, but I want to see the Hoover Dam."

"Really?" I laugh because I figured the Bellagio fountain show, Caesar's Palace, the roller coasters at Stratosphere would be high on her list. But the dam? I shrug. "Okay."

We walk into the hotel room, and I drop our bags on the luggage rack then tackle her to the bed.

"I feel dirty from flying," she says.

"You'll be dirty once I'm done with you." I attack her neck.

She puts her hand on my chest and pushes me back. "Shower sex?"

I bounce up onto my feet, offering her my hand. "You speak my language."

After turning on the water, I strip off her shirt and unclip her bra from the front. The weight of her breasts pulls the fabric, and I run my hands over her, nudging them free.

"I love your tits." I lean forward and kiss her.

"Is it bad that I can't wait to be loud?"

I bite her bottom lip, pulling it out and letting it go with a pop. "Make the walls shake, baby."

I push her yoga pants down her body, along with her panties. I hold open the glass shower door and lead her inside, allowing her to enjoy the warmth of the water while I strip. Then I join her, corner her, and push one leg up. It didn't take me long to figure out that one of the great things about having a girlfriend is the fact that I don't have to wear a condom. We can do it when and wherever we want. I slide right into her and she's soaked, as though she's been waiting for this all day.

I find out something new about Frankie in that shower—she's pretty damn loud when she's allowed to be.

AN HOUR after our shower sex, we're in a rental car, driving toward Hoover Dam.

Frankie's almost giddy next to me, which is ten times better than she was on the plane, but weird at the same time.

"Why the Hoover Dam?" I ask.

She looks out the window. "I'm not saying."

"What? Why not?" Her vagueness only intrigues me more.

"You're going to make fun of me."

"I will not. I never even mention the puking in my lap thing."

She lightly smacks my chest. "You just did."

"Only to prove my point."

She situates herself so she's more facing me than looking out the window. I put my hand on her knee. I swear I can't stop touching her.

Finally she says, "When I was younger, I loved that movie, *Fools Rush In*. She throws a coin for good luck when she crosses the state border. There."

I can't fight the laughter pouring out of me. "Frankie Grant is a romantic?"

She rolls her eyes, huffs, and straightens to look out the window.

I grab her leg and shake it. "It's okay. You're a woman, of course you are."

She rolls her eyes again. "She threw the coin, then she met Matthew Perry's character, went home with him, and she got pregnant."

I laugh harder. "So they got together because she was pregnant? Maybe not such a romantic then."

Her death glare returns. "No. They came from different worlds."

"Let me guess, one of them was poor?" See? Every damn movie.

"No. I mean, he was rich, but she wasn't poor."

"Was she rich?" I ask.

"No. *Ugh*." She clenches her fists. "It's a good movie, and it used to make me think about how I didn't have to stay in Wisconsin and marry someone from my own town. That I could find love somewhere else."

I shake her thigh again and she glares out the window. "Then I'm glad, because I was never going to venture to Wisconsin, that's for sure."

"Hey, there's nothing wrong with Wisconsin, okay?"

"What do they have besides cows and cheese?"

"That's like saying all New York has is bagels and pizza," she says.

"And I'm proud to come from a place that mastered those two things. You should be proud to come from cheese."

She shakes her head. I love baiting her. It's way too much fun.

"I'm going to drag you there sometime." She acts as if that's a threat.

Truthfully, I'm not a meet-the-parents type of guy, but it's one of the good things about her having a strained relationship with her parents—I won't have to meet them.

"For some cheese and milk?"

She playfully smacks me. If we weren't on a highway, I'd kiss her right now.

Our conversation turns to inking and how nervous she is about tomorrow. As much as I try to relax her, I understand her nerves. I almost threw up before my first pop-up event. Tattooing people on the fly when you didn't work with them for weeks, perfecting exactly what they want, is nerve-wracking. But she'll kill it, I know she will.

We park at Hoover Dam. When Frankie finds out we have to park and walk across where Arizona and Nevada come together, not drive over, it's like her dream was shot.

"Come on, you can still throw a coin over," I say and tug her toward the street.

"It's not like in the movie."

"Real life rarely is."

She shakes her head, and I pull her into my arms, kissing her briefly because there are families around.

We reach the middle of the dam and I step over the line and say, "I'm in a different state than you."

She pushes me. It's fun being silly with her. I slide a coin into her palm, and she smiles at me, holding it up.

"Kiss it," she says.

I kiss the metal and she looks around before tossing it over the edge of the dam.

"Good luck, huh?"

"A little luck never hurt anyone," she says.

I wrap my arms around her middle, her head falls to my shoulder, and we stare over the edge. She's right that a little luck never hurt anyone, but I have a hard time believing me kissing a coin and her tossing it into the water will bring us good luck. But I won't tell her that. I won't pop that bubble for her. God knows it hurt when people popped mine.

I hold her close, my eyes closed, and inhale her scent—dreading the moment when I blow this all up. Things in my life are way too good right now. Surely something will happen. It always does.

She turns her head and kisses my jaw. "Thank you for bringing me."

"Hey, the Hoover Dam is cool."

"No, Jax." She swivels in my arms. "To Vegas. I know what you're doing, and I appreciate you giving me a small taste of what it would've been like had I made different choices, but I want you to know, I'm happy in Cliffton Heights. I'm happy having Jolie, Ink Envy, and you."

She kisses me, and that feeling of dread weighs me down even more.

Don't put your faith and happiness on me, Frankie. That's gotta be a mistake.

CHAPTER TWENTY-FOUR

Frankie

*T*he next morning, Jax wakes me by sliding down between my legs. Since we always sleep separately at home, it's nice to be in his arms the entire night and not have to worry about Jolie walking in.

I call home. Jolie's with Sandy since Saturday is a busy day for Rian and Dylan, and she tells me they're going ice skating.

Then Jax takes me to a breakfast place he swears by, and I make him stop at the M&M store. Sometimes I worry I'm domesticating him sooner than he's ready for. Like, if I didn't have Jolie and we were a couple, we would've gambled last night and gone out to the clubs. But I've been done with that scene for a long time. Once you have to take care of a child the next day, the night before doesn't seem quite as worth it.

After breakfast, he walks me over to the expo place. Immediately, someone is calling his name. We both turn to find a big guy waving at us. He's got a few other guys with him, and they all smile and wave as if they know Jax.

"Owens!" The big guy smacks Jax's hand in a handshake. "Damn, you just disappeared. I half thought you'd be MIA tonight."

"If I say I'll be here, I will." Jax's reaction isn't jovial in any way.

"Well, I'm guessing this is Frankie Grant?" He puts his hand out to me, and I shake it.

"Yes," I say.

Jax says, "Frankie, this is the owner, Logan, and that's Timmy and Jimmy behind him. They're the ones who put the whole thing together."

I shake all their hands.

"Let me show you where you'll be." Logan waves us forward.

I try to distinguish the tats on his head, but they look like a design of some kind. The guy's probably had crazy talented artists do his ink if he owns this place. It's a tattoo museum of sorts and is known for bringing in tattoo artists from all over the world every weekend.

We come up to what's more or less a glass booth that we'll be in. It's set on one end of the room and you can see in from all angles except the back. There's a big banner with Jax's name and mine, the exact same size as though we're equals. The picture that Jax took of me and sent in is on there too. It's weird seeing my face and name as if I'm some celebrity.

"Usually we only have one artist, so we had to improvise." Logan looks at me.

Jax walks into the glass room, looking at the setup as though he's making sure it meets his final approval.

"We were surprised you were ready to bring in some competition," Jimmy says.

Timmy shoots him a "shut the fuck up" look. But either Jimmy doesn't see it or doesn't care because he looks at me.

"Shut up, Jimmy," Logan says.

Jax doesn't respond, so maybe he didn't hear Jimmy. "What do you think, Frankie? Enough room?"

They've divided the room with two chairs far enough apart to keep everything sanitary.

"The only ones in the room are you and the client," Logan says.

"And if the client wants privacy?" I ask.

Logan looks at Jax, not nearly as happy to answer me. "There's one bench behind that curtain, but it's all glass so people can watch you. And it's not only people who have booked. There are other tattoo artists who like to check out your skills." Logan sets his eyes on me. "You ready for that?"

Jax puts his arm around me as though he's staking some claim. "She's more than ready—and talented."

"Oh!" Jimmy points at us. "You're fucking her. That's why she's here."

"Shut up, Jimmy," Logan warns.

Again, Jax has no reaction. I thought for sure he'd be ready to beat the shit out of the guy.

"I brought her because she's good and people will love her work." He slides his arm around my back and takes my hand. "We're going to look around. We'll bring our stuff tonight. What time do you want us?"

"You've got a long list of people. We booked your first clients at seven."

Jax nods. "Cool. We'll be here. Thanks, guys."

"Thank you," I say quickly before Jax drags me away. I look over my shoulder to see the three of them staring at us as we walk away. "We could've had lunch or something with your friends."

"They aren't my friends. They just want the money I'm

about to bring in tonight." He looks at me. "The money *we're* going to bring in."

I have to walk fast to keep up with him. "I don't think they like that I came with you."

He shakes his head. "I don't give a shit what they like. Just wait until they see your work. They'll be begging to book you over me."

I shake my head—he's wrong on that one.

We tour the building, walking through rooms that talk about the origins of tattooing. There's even a display with pictures of full arm sleeves and you have to guess who they belong to. Weirdly, Jax is on there. I think because no one in Cliffton Heights knows him that well, I forget that it's not that way everywhere. He's made a name for himself in this world—and that's when I realize that maybe I haven't fully prepared myself for what's going to happen tonight. What if his line is super long and my line has no one? I love watching Jax ink, but not when I'm supposed to be working too.

Suddenly fear grips my throat and I have a hard time breathing.

"You okay?" Jax leans over.

I swallow and nod. "Yeah, just nerves."

"Come here." He tugs on my sleeve and brings me over to a sign that says, "The Tattoo Museum." "Ready?"

He poses us for a selfie and snaps it, types something on his phone, and a second later, my phone dings with an Instagram notification.

He's tagged me in the picture. Likes are already piling up.

"Don't you want this life again? Don't you miss it?" I ask.

He shakes his head. "No. Not at all. I'm a little annoyed right now."

"I thought you might say something to that Jimmy guy."

He looks at me for a second. "He's an idiot. The man has no talent and that's why his mouth is attached to Logan's ass.

191

He's not a threat, but even if he was, I don't handle my shit like that." He steps closer, his hand cradling my cheek. "I'm not violent. I know I hit Michael, but that's because of what he did to you."

I nod. "I know you're not, but I guess I just assume that'll be the reaction because it's what I'm used to."

"Jax Owens, back in Vegas. It's been a long time."

I weave to look behind him and find a cute tatted-up pink-haired woman with a short skirt and halter top showing off a belly button piercing.

Jax circles and holds my hand. "Reese."

"You act like you're not happy to see me. Like you didn't think I'd be here." She walks across the room as if she's on a catwalk. "I heard about your girl." She puts her hand out between us. "Frankie, right?"

"Yeah." I shake her hand, still trying to get a read on this situation.

"Frankie, this is Reese. She's like Jimmy," Jax says, implying that she's no good at tattooing either.

"Logan keeps some of his special people in-house," Reese says, flipping her hair. "I saw you on Instagram. Cute pic. Your work is interesting."

I say nothing but bite down my smile because she's trying to bait me and I'm not going to take it. I'm here for the weekend and that's all.

"Thanks." I look her body over. Her ink is decent, but I can tell she's let one too many people work on her. "I like your butterfly."

"Oh, that's Jax's handiwork. He also did this one." She lifts her shirt, exposing her tit to show me a row of butterflies all over one breast as though they're flying away.

"Jesus, Reese," Jax says. "Put your damn shirt down."

I do my best to hide my irritation. "Jax is talented."

She nods. "He is. At more than just tattooing." She grins and looks him over.

"Christ, Reese, she gets the point. We used to fuck. Now move on with whatever else you have to say."

I'm glad Jax at least called her out.

"Nothing," Reese says. "I'm just surprised to see you. Are you done living like a monk? Coming back to real life?" She looks at me as if I'm some piece of trash he's been sleeping with.

"We're all adults here. You can come right out and say whatever it is you want to say." I raise my eyebrows at her.

"Let's go." Jax tugs at my hand, but I keep my feet planted.

"Jax has way too much talent to be hiding in some small town. It's great that he found someone to keep his dick wet while he was there, but we're ready for him to come home."

"Home? This is his home?" I gesture around us.

She cocks her hip out and crosses her arms, so her tits are on display. I don't have the heart to look at Jax to see if he notices. I'm sure he does.

"I guess that's his decision to make. But just a warning..." I lean in closer. "Just because you hang out with talented people doesn't make you talented. Do you think I didn't stalk your Instagram before we got here? I've seen your work. It's really promising—for a novice." I pat her on the back. "Keep up the good work, Reese." I look at Jax. "I'll be outside when you're ready."

I'm not really a badass. People think I am because I have that "don't fuck with me" chip on my shoulder, but truth is, I never checked Instagram and I had no idea about Reese. From the way she's all protective of him, she must've thought there was something more between them. Or maybe he did too. Everything I know about Jax says I'm his first real relationship, but I only know what he tells me. Bringing me to the big question—do I trust Jax?

He comes out five minutes later. "Want to walk to the hotel? I need a breather."

"Sure."

We've walked for about ten minutes, dodging the tourists, when he finally speaks again. "It was never serious with us."

"Okay." I smile on the outside because I don't want him to think I needed the reassurance. How weak would that make me seem?

"It was just sex."

"I said okay." I clamp my teeth together because I do not want to hear about my boyfriend's sex life with some other chick.

"So you're good? Not jealous?" he asks.

I ignore the green liquid running through my veins. "Nope." I leave it to one-word responses so as not to give myself away.

He stops us at the corner light. "You sure?"

I nod. "Totally. I mean... we all have our pasts."

He kisses me, takes my hand, and leads us back to the hotel. Once the hotel room door shuts, he fucks me so long and so hard that the fear that he's thinking of Reese and not me trickles in.

Jesus, Frankie, do not ruin this for yourself. Jax has done nothing but show you that you can trust him.

CHAPTER TWENTY-FIVE

Jax

"You're wearing that?" I stare at Frankie's ass in a snug pair of black leather pants.

She stops applying her makeup and turns around. "Yeah, why?"

"Because I'd like to be able to pay attention to my clients and not want to beat down every guy who's checking you out." I break the distance between us, placing my hands on the smooth leather rounding her hips. "Your ass looks so good I want to take a bite."

She leans forward to continue applying her mascara.

"Perfect position." I thrust my growing dick into her ass.

"Jax, you're gonna make me mess up my makeup."

I thrust into her ass again, and my dick gets harder.

"Put it away, we don't have time," she says.

I've already fucked her twice today—the second time was after we saw Reese. I'm happy Frankie wasn't jealous of

Reese—because she should feel confident in us—but damn, she didn't blink an eye.

"Are you sure you don't want to wear something else?" I ask.

She turns around and I take in her shirt that reveals her stomach. The stomach I purposely came all over this afternoon as some caveman claim that she was mine.

"Goddamn, I should just ice my knuckles now in preparation."

She giggles and pushes me back. "Stop it. Let's go."

Her phone rings right as she's putting it into her purse. I snatch it up, thinking it's Jolie, but the name Aiden flashes on the screen. Who the fuck is Aiden?

"Here you go." I hand it to her.

When she sees the name, she squeals and slides her finger over the screen. What am I missing? She walks away from me and I act as if I don't care as I lie on the bed, but one ear is on her conversation.

"Aiden!"

"Shut up?"

"Seriously?"

"You're here?"

I groan. *Why are we excited some other guy is here?*

"Yeah, I'll be there."

"I could totally use a friendly face."

Um, hello, I'm a friendly face.

"Can you get in?"

"That might not impress them.

"Yeah, let me talk to Jax."

Great. Now she's going to ask me to get some guy into the event.

"It's new."

"She's good. She's home though, with Michael's mom and some of our friends."

"She would have loved that."

"Okay, great. How many of you are there?"

"I'll let Jax know. I'm sure it's fine. I'll call if there's a problem."

"You too. I'm so excited."

Should we all do a happy dance that Aiden is in Vegas? I think not.

"See you tonight." She hangs up and jumps on the bed, crawls up on her knees, and her smile couldn't be pulled off her face, it's so big and wide. "That was Aiden."

"I heard."

"He's my cousin, and he's in town with two of his friends. He saw our Instagram picture."

I nod. The relief that washes through me should probably concern me.

"And I haven't seen him in so long. He plays hockey for the Florida Fury and I'm not sure, but is that enough to get him tickets?"

I sit up straighter. "Wait. Your cousin is Aiden Drake? Why am I just now finding this out?"

She nods. "Do you follow hockey?"

"I did before *Paw Patrol* took over my television."

She giggles. "Do you think you can get him in?"

I pull my phone out of my pocket and message Logan that Aiden Drake needs an in plus two. I know he'll do it. Anything that gets his place on the lips of more people. "He's in."

"Thank you," she says and hugs me.

I take advantage of the moment and grab her ass with both hands. "Quickie?"

"You'll ruin my makeup. You have me all night once it's over." She slides off me, and my dick and I have a little pity party, commiserating together. "Come on. I don't want to be late."

I roll off the bed and grab our bags before we leave the hotel room. We arrive at the museum and there's already a line to get in, so we slide in through the side entrance.

As we each prepare our workspaces, I can't help but check out Frankie. Her smile almost makes me happy to be here. I didn't think I'd want to come here again, but I booked it with Logan as a final thank you for everything he did for me. But being back in this atmosphere again, I'm annoyed and remembering how used I felt when I left. Now they have the audacity to make fun of Cliffton Heights? Then there's Reese saying I'm too good to be in that town. Hell, she only wanted me for what it got her.

But I see Frankie enjoying tonight, and I worry she'll want to do more. Sadly, this is my last one. After this, I'm done. If someone wants a tattoo, they'll have to book me at Ink Envy.

"I'm so excited." Frankie comes over and sits on my lap once she's done with her setup. I kiss the nape of her neck. "I'm nervous though."

My hand falls between her legs. "You know an orgasm is the perfect way to make those nerves go away?"

"Really?" She stands and takes my hand. "You are the expert in this area. I might need you to show me."

She pulls me behind the black curtain, and I flip the button of her leather pants while she palms my hard-on through my jeans. Damn, we're going to have to sanitize this bench again.

Logan comes in and announces each of us as if we're rock stars. I knew he'd never make Frankie seem less than, because he wants people to spend money and they won't spend money on someone they don't think is the best out there. After tonight, Logan will see he was mistaken for questioning Frankie.

I'm not sure if it was planned or just coincidence that I get a woman and she gets a man right off the bat. My client wants a heart I designed on her pelvis, so she has to unbutton her pants, whereas Frankie's guy gets his on his bicep.

She looks at the faces plastered to the wall but buries her head, working on the tattoo. Once the music starts, Frankie does what she does best. She works and makes her client feel comfortable. Having conversations with everyone, talking about Jolie—turns out I miss the little girl a lot—so I join in talking about how awesome her daughter is.

Most of the time, it's the two of us talking with our clients about anything from what someone did on the Strip, to where they're from, or our personal lives. This is what I miss most, but I have this in Cliffton Heights too. Maybe if I always had Frankie with me, this atmosphere would be tolerable.

Midway through the night, when my hands are cramping, Aiden Drake taps on the glass. Frankie smiles and waves to her cousin. He's with two other guys.

"We have a break in ten," I tell her, and she puts up ten fingers so Aiden knows how long it will be.

"I'd never heard of you," Frankie's client says. "But when I looked you up, I saw that Hennessy uses you, huh?"

Frankie dips her gun. "Only for her holistic designs, but she's been my client for a while."

"I think she's been keeping you a secret on purpose."

Frankie laughs, but I could see it. Some people don't think tattoo artists can design an array of different things, and they don't want a copy-and-paste tattoo on other people.

"I follow her. One time she got this tattoo done by Choi." The girl looks at me because she's done her research and clearly knows I did my apprenticeship under Choi. "I tried to get in to see him, but I have a better chance of winning the lottery."

"He really only does his regulars now," I say.

The girl smiles at Frankie. "Maybe you'll be my new tattoo artist. I do love Hennessy."

And so it begins. The whole "if you're good enough for so and so, you're good enough for me."

We finish the tattoos, and Jimmy tells everyone we're taking a break. His brother Timmy brings us some food.

"Hey, Jimmy, those three guys can come in," I say, pointing at Frankie's cousin.

Aiden and his buddies make their way through the crowd, and Jimmy lets them pass him while all the people groan and ask why they're allowed in.

"Because Jax said so," Jimmy says, passing the buck off to me.

"Aiden!" Frankie stands and rushes toward him. They look nothing alike.

"Hey. How are you?"

She leaves his arms and steps back. "This is Jax." She waits for me to come forward.

I put my hand out to shake his. Aiden's handshake is firm, and he gives me the once-over. "Hey, Jax. This is Maksim and Ford."

I nod. "I know. It's great to meet you. Frankie's been keeping the fact her cousin is a hockey player under wraps." I'm doing my best not to fanboy in their presence, but I'm not sure whether I'm succeeding.

Aiden almost looks sheepish. "I can guess why. We're both the black sheep of our families." He winks at her, and she smiles.

I sit on a table and open our bag of food. "Are you guys hungry?"

Maksim steps forward, and Aiden puts his hand out to stop him. "No, we're good."

The Ford guy is looking at my arm as though he wishes he had a magnifying glass. "We saw that arm downstairs. You're pretty well-known, I take it?"

Frankie laughs. "Jax is very well-known in the industry."

Ford looks around. "I had no idea there were these things. I mean, I know there's been some reality shows on tattoo artists, but this is like your own little world."

"You have to excuse Ford. He comes from the land of the rich and famous." Aiden uses a fake uppity accent.

"You're from New York?" I ask Ford, recognizing his slight accent.

He nods. "Yeah, you too?"

"Yeah, but pretty sure we didn't travel in the same circles." I chuckle.

"Which is why I had no idea you could be a tattoo celebrity."

Maksim lifts his shirt in front of Frankie. "What do you suggest?"

Frankie laughs. "Um… whatever you want, but I'm not sure I can do it now. But you guys should come to Cliffton Heights next time you're playing in New York." She touches Aiden's arm. "You can see Jolie."

"Show me some pics?" Aiden asks and sits next to Frankie.

I glance between his friends. Both Maksim and Aiden have ink, so I say to Ford, "You have any tats?" He shakes his head. "You're the only one out of your friends without tats, huh? We could pop your cherry this weekend."

"I thought we were all booked?" Frankie asks.

"I'm sure I can squeeze you in," I tell Ford.

"I have no idea what I'd get."

"A tribal band?" I joke, and Maksim laughs along with me. "Whatever speaks to you." I shrug.

"I suggest for the first one, you really think about it. Jax can sketch something and make it personal," Frankie pipes in with her opinion.

I look at Aiden's arm tattoo and ask Frankie, "Yours?"

"I really should touch that up, Aid. You trusted me before I knew what I was doing."

Aiden laughs. "I love it. And the fact that you did it."

It's good work. Sure, it might not be as original as she is now, but everyone starts somewhere when they're developing their talent. She has a specialty she's perfected now, but I'm not sure Aiden is the type of guy to sport a holistic tattoo.

"Tattoos are supposed to speak to the person and those ones seem like they fit you?" I ask Aiden.

"Thank you, Jax." He points at me. "I like him."

Frankie looks at me, and I can't stop myself from bending down and kissing her.

Jimmy walks in. "Time's up, guys."

"Oh, I haven't even eaten." Frankie opens the bag and grabs a fry.

"We're going to hit a club. Want to meet us after?" Ford asks. "You used your clout for us, let us use ours for you."

Frankie looks over. Although I'd love to crash in our room and order room service, I'm sure she wants to spend more time with her cousin.

I shrug. "I'm game."

Frankie smiles. "We'll text you when we're out of here."

"Great. See you in a bit." Aiden hugs Frankie.

Maksim and Ford must see themselves as family because they hug her too.

Huh. This isn't a hugging booth, assholes.

After I wave goodbye and she comes back to her station, I

hook a finger in the loop of her pants and pull her toward me. "These pants are driving me crazy."

"I know. I only wore them for you." She kisses me briefly and walks over to her station, glancing over her shoulder to see if I'm looking. Of course I'm looking.

CHAPTER TWENTY-SIX

Frankie

*J*ax is asked by at least ten people where he'll be after we're done. He mostly brushes them off, telling them vaguely that we'll be at a lot of clubs. Aiden has already texted me where to meet him.

My feet are killing me in these heels, and although I love that my leather pants are driving Jax crazy, I just want a pair of pajama pants and a cart of room service. But this is Jax's life here. I don't want him to think I can't hang with him.

After we're done, Logan comes in and places money on both of our tables. "Everyone loved it. I could have you guys once a month and I'm not sure the crowd would tire of you. One girl told Jimmy you two were her new best friends." He shakes his head. "I had my doubts about this when Jax called. I thought, is pussy really this important? But I guess there're still some hidden gems in Small Town, USA, huh?"

I huff. Jax smirks at me with a grin so big he doesn't have to say the words "I told you so."

"Thank you for having me, Logan." I take the cash and kiss his cheek.

He turns to Jax. "Can I have a word?"

I look at Jax as that smirk is stripped from his face. "Give us a minute, Frankie. I'll grab your bag."

"Okay."

I walk out of the small glass tattoo room. Although I have no idea what Logan wants to talk to Jax about, I'm happy about how tonight went. It was so much fun tattooing alongside Jax, meeting people I never would have, traveling to a new place. I could see it becoming addicting. As I linger, checking out some of the displays again, Reese approaches me.

She pretends she's reading what I am on the wall. "You know you can't play house with a guy like Jax, right?"

"We're not playing at anything," I say.

"Sure, you are. I found you and your friends online. A little girl, huh? Is that how you trapped him into liking you? Using your daughter to lure him in?"

I turn to face her and narrow my eyes. "Don't talk about my daughter. And whatever is between us is none of your business."

"It kind of is because I consider Jax a friend. More than a friend actually, and if you're pulling the wool over his eyes, he deserves to know."

"I hate to break it to you, but Jax doesn't feel the same about you." I pat her on the shoulder.

She brushes it off. "You might have him now, but we both know you can't keep up with him. What are you gonna do once he's done feeling like being some loser-ass dad in a small town? Get pregnant? Trap him?"

"Listen. I'm sorry if he did you wrong. You're obviously

holding on to some hostility but pushing bullshit theories on me isn't going to work. I have no chain attached to him. He's free to leave whenever he wants."

I turn to walk away, but she takes my wrist and flips me around. "He's only going to break your heart. Do you think he didn't use that foster kid story on me? Did he tell you how he doesn't do relationships but then sticks around to lead you on? Hell, I wasn't the first and you won't be the last. It's called getting laid. I thought you looked smarter than that."

What is it with mean girls? Do they go to a special school to figure out your biggest fear and exploit it? Damn. Of course I've felt that Jax and I fell together in some ways because of Jolie. If he didn't fall so hard for her, maybe our lives wouldn't have weaved together. But those insecurities come from being a single mother.

"What's going on?" Jax says from behind me. "Reese, how nice of you to hang around. You never did get the point very easily, did you?"

She smiles with her perfect white teeth. "I'm just enlightening Frankie. This scene is all so new to her."

"I'm sure you are," he says and looks at me. "Ready?"

I nod.

"Bye, Reese. See you... never again." I give her a saccharine smile.

We walk away, and when he stoops to grab our bags, I look over my shoulder. Reese is still there, smiling, and I'm ninety percent sure she's fucking with me. If only there wasn't that ten percent that worries she's telling the truth.

"Did you hear from Aiden?" Jax asks.

"Yeah."

"Okay, we'll drop these at the front desk of the hotel, then meet them wherever they're at."

I smile and nod. I'd rather let Jax prove to me that Reese is wrong while he makes love to me, but I haven't seen Aiden in forever. And I could use a distraction from this other life of Jax's, so cousin time wins out.

THE CLUB IS dark and sweaty and everything I don't enjoy anymore. Did I really age out of the club scene so young?

Jax follows me as I weave through the people, their skin sticking to mine as I pass by. By the time I get to the roped-off VIP section, Ford is popping open a bottle of champagne.

"Our famous friends!" Ford yells, and a splash of the champagne douses a girl's blouse. She's too drunk to care, I think, because she just laughs.

God, I'm so over this scene.

We walk through the ropes, and Jax shakes their hands again, asking the waitress for a whiskey. I've only ever seen him drink hard alcohol when something big is on his mind. Did something happen with Logan?

"I'll have club soda and lime," I tell her.

"Club soda?" Ford yells. "Aiden, what's up with your cousin?"

Aiden dislodges himself from a huddle of girls. "She can get whatever she wants."

"I'm off drinking after an embarrassing situation." I look at Jax.

He shakes his head and kisses my cheek. "As long as there are no drinking games, we should be okay."

It could be me, or maybe it's him, but since we left the museum, it's like we're robots going through the motions of what a couple does.

We sit in the booth and Aiden sits with us.

"You know you don't have to keep us company," I tell Aiden.

"This scene is getting boring. Ford dragged me here because, as you can tell, he loves it."

Sure enough, Ford has three women around him, all touching him as if it's some game of whose hand gives Ford the hard-on.

"You've really turned your year around these past few weeks," Jax says.

I wish I followed hockey, but as Jax mentioned, I can name all the *Paw Patrol* characters but not much else.

Aiden nods. "I was in a slump and I'm not sure I'm out of it yet, but I found something that's working."

"Like a superstition?" Jax asks.

He shrugs. "More like a good luck charm."

"Do tell, little cousin." I lean forward and so does Jax.

The music grows louder, but he tells us, and I think we both heard him right, which sounds absolutely ridiculous.

"Whatever works," Jax says and drinks his whiskey.

"What is this? Get off your ass and dance." Maksim comes over. "Do you mind, Jax?"

"I'm not dancing," I say.

"With an outfit like that, you are." Maksim doesn't lower his hand. His Russian accent makes it sound more like an order than a request.

"He's harmless. If it were Ford, I'd tell you to say hell no, but Maksim just likes to dance," Aiden tells Jax.

Jax slides out of the booth, allowing me to get out. I kiss Jax and follow Maksim to the dance floor. Most of the women are wearing half the clothes I am, and I feel like exactly what I am—a mom.

But then a good song with a catchy beat comes on and I can't help but dance with Maksim. Aiden wasn't kidding—the kid is everywhere, like he's a magnet and everyone wants in on his energy. Women, men, and even one of the waitresses stop and dance with him. I'm so busy laughing I don't even bother to consider how I'm dancing.

He twirls me and pulls me back. His hips shake and his ass circles, he squats down at me, his hands never touching me, but he is eye level with my pussy for longer than a minute.

Ford comes out and joins our duo. Now there are more women rubbing their bodies along not just Maksim and Ford but me. A redhead gives me the eye and thrusts her pelvis to my ass. It's all just fun, and song by song goes by as I lose myself in the circle. The fear and everything about Jax and Jolie and Michael disappears as though someone slipped me a magic drug that makes all my worries fade away. I never realized how scared I was about this thing with Jax until it's not front and center in my mind.

Ford grabs my hips and puts his leg between my legs, but I push him away and put my finger up in the air. He looks back at our section where Jax is talking to Aiden.

"He'll kick your ass," I yell. He probably won't because he's not a violent guy, but it's an easy way to get Ford off of me.

"He's not even paying attention," he says.

I shake my head. "One day you're going to learn a very important lesson."

"And what's that?" he yells above the pounding music.

"Not to play with matches. I think you're the type who likes to fire off little sparks everywhere. One day it's going to burn you."

A girl comes over, and I realize I'm lecturing a guy who just wants to get laid. I'm sweaty and I bet my makeup is dripping off me, so I look around and head to the restroom.

On my way there, someone pulls me back into his body. His hand slides around my waist, but I don't remove it. I'd recognize that calloused forefinger and thumb, not to mention his scent, anywhere.

"You're driving me crazy. I'm about to kick that Ford guy's ass," Jax says in my ear.

I shouldn't smile that he's jealous. That would be immature. But I do anyway.

I twist in his arms and wind my own around his neck. "I want to go to the hotel."

"You're speaking my language. Want to say goodbye to Aiden?" he asks.

"Give me a second." I wind my way back through the crowd. I lean down beside my cousin so he can hear me. "We're leaving. I'm too old for this."

Aiden laughs. "I'm too old for this too. It's good to see you. Come down to Florida and show Jolie the ocean."

I hug him tightly. He's one of my only connections to my family. "Deal. Keep that lucky charm, okay?"

He rolls his eyes. "As long as I keep scoring."

"Bye, Aiden," I say.

"See you. He's a good guy," he says with a nod.

I glance over my shoulder at Jax. "I know."

Just as I'm about to move, Aiden grips my hand to stop me. I lean in closer to hear over the music. "Don't let your past dictate your future, okay? That's my unsolicited advice. Forget all the shit with Michael. Start fresh."

I hug him one more time, squeezing him extra hard. "Thank you. Love you."

"Love you back."

I walk out of the roped-off area, and Jax takes my hand, leading me out of the club. Once we're outside, he backs me up against a wall and kisses me until I can barely stand.

"I need to get you back to the hotel before I fuck you right here," Jax says.

I step away and flag down a taxi.

"I do love a take-charge woman," he says and opens the door of the taxi that stops.

I slide in, but Jax's lips work mine, and I don't remember anything about the ride back to the hotel or the elevator ride up. When the door shuts and we're in our own private oasis, I finally feel at peace again.

CHAPTER TWENTY-SEVEN

Jax

*O*nce the hotel room door clicks shut, I flip the deadbolt and the bar over, then turn to face Frankie.

"It made me crazy watching you with Ford," I shamelessly admit. I put my arms around her stomach, unbuttoning her leather pants. "I'm not usually a jealous man, but these pants made me see red, knowing any guy in there would be thinking of exactly what I plan on doing to you right now."

Her head falls back, and she doesn't stop my hand from sliding down past the waistband of her panties. "Reese said some shit."

I knew she did. I could tell. Normally it would bother me that a woman wasn't secure enough not to question whatever we have, but I understand what Frankie has been through. Plus, this whole life I had before her isn't anything she's used to.

"She's a liar. Whatever she said."

Her arm wraps around my neck, and she kisses my jawline. "She said your line about not wanting a commitment is an act. That you've told a lot of women that."

I slide my hand out from her delicious pussy and look her straight in the eye. "She's lying. It's not an act. I think that's why Ford made me so jealous. He probably grew up with a silver spoon in his mouth, and he deserves you. I don't."

"Don't say that." Her hands fall to my cheeks.

"I have nothing to offer you except a birth certificate with a dead mom listed. I have no idea if I have some hereditary heart condition and could collapse tomorrow or if cancer runs in my family." *Turn off the faucet, man, stop pouring everything out to her.* But no matter how much my inner dialogue says to stop, I continue. "I am screwed up and it scares me because I'm loving this... whatever this is between us."

"Is it because of Jolie?" A single tear slips from her eye. "The reason why you started to have feelings. Is it because you love Jolie?"

I shake my head and brush her tear away. What is she thinking? Goddamn Reese. "No. God, Frankie, you honestly thought I didn't like *you*? Would anybody else buy a whole case of T-shirts just to get your attention? The minute I found you in Rian's apartment, I knew I was in trouble. Jolie could win over an old Catholic school nun, it's true. But you? All the shit I gave you was a sad attempt to get your attention. I knew you were going through things and I just liked to distract you from it all."

"Really?"

I nod. "This is where you tell me you've had the hots for me this whole time."

She giggles. "When you had that talk with Dylan about him pursuing Rian, it did make me pretty hot for you. And watching you with Jolie and now Gumdrop might have upped your hotness factor a little."

I dip my head to look into her eyes. "A little?"

"A lot. God, Jax, why are we so insecure with one another?" She walks over to the bed and slides up it, bringing her knees to her chest. "What does that say about us?"

"It says we both care about how this turns out. Maybe we rushed this. It's early and maybe with time…"

She tilts her head. "I wish I had met you before Michael."

Does she really think that would fix this?

"No, you don't," I say.

"Why not?"

"You wouldn't have Jolie. And as much as I'm pretty sure we would have an awesome kid, Jolie is the coolest little girl around. Plus, if we had to get together before people fucked up our psyches, we'd have had to have met just after I left the hospital after being born and that's a little sick." She laughs and I put my arm around her. "So neither one of us has to be jealous, right?"

"I have one more confession," she says.

"What's that?"

"I don't like clubbing anymore. I would have rather come here and ordered room service."

I laugh and lean over her, grabbing the room service guide. "Me too. Order away."

She takes the menu but puts it on the side of the bed. "In a minute." She straddles me and I rest my hands on her hips. "What did Logan tell you?"

"He wanted me to come back on a permanent basis."

Her shoulders sink.

"But I told him I'm done with this life. I know that my friends here don't understand my reasons and I don't really care. If you want to do pop-up shows, I'll totally help you. I loved working side by side with you tonight, but we do that every day. And that's enough for me." She kisses me, and when she closes the kiss, I say, "I take it that's a good thing?"

"The best. I loved that I got to experience it, but I'm happy back home too."

I roll us over and push her hair off her face so I can kiss her again. Our tongues meet and slide together. The more she moans, the harder I get. I open her shirt, exposing her tits that I visualized long before I ever saw them bare.

Her hands caress me, pulling up the back of my shirt, urging me to take it off. I break from sucking on her nipples to take off my shirt, then slide her leather pants and her panties down her body. She inches up, and as she unbuttons my pants, she kisses my stomach and my fingers weave through her hair.

Tonight the energy between us feels different after putting everything on the table.

Once we're naked, I urge her to climb up onto the bed and use my knee to open her thighs and make a spot for me to nestle between them.

"Oh, Jax," she says, staring into my eyes.

This woman has ruined me completely. Her way of opening all her wounds and trusting me to be the one who heals them feels like the most precious gift I've ever been blessed with. I've never been more scared but honored at the same time.

The tip of my dick pierces her opening, and she raises her legs to give me more room, allowing me to slide in. She moans from the sensation of me inside her. I've never made love to anyone, but as I circle my hips, I can't help but look her in the eye, hoping to dissolve all her worries. To prove that two hurt people can heal—together and apart. Neither one of us has to save the other, but we can save each other.

Her hands slide down my back, and she pulls at my shoulder blades when I thrust harder and grind deeper.

"It feels so good," she says.

I place my forearms on either side of her head to hold my weight off her while I dust her face with kisses. Her forehead, her nose, her lips.

I groan, sliding in and out of her, and just when she gets that look in her eye and she bucks into me mid-thrust, I crash my lips to hers, pouring every feeling I have for her into the kiss. She's changed me. I'll never be the person I was before her.

She strips her mouth from mine on a breathy moan. "I'm gonna come."

Sweat forms between our bodies and I hold one of her legs up to get deeper inside her. She cries out a moment later, and I continue going until my orgasm crests a minute later.

I don't draw out of her right away, but instead we kiss, and our hands roam over one another's body as though we're cherishing the final notes of the last song of the night.

An hour later, I'm in a hotel robe when there's a knock on the door. Two guys come in with room service carts, and I sign and tip them.

After they leave, Frankie comes out of the bathroom and climbs on the bed. "Oh, you do know your way to my heart." She lifts the cloche lids, growing more excited with each one.

I get on the bed next to her, and we watch television and eat room service for the rest of the night. It's not an eventful night, but it's one of the best ones I've ever had. I finally feel as though a weight has been lifted off of me.

CHAPTER TWENTY-EIGHT

Frankie

*T*he Uber parks along the curb, and I don't wait for it to fully stop before I open the door and run into Ink Envy. Jolie's there, teaching Gumdrop to lie down. Her head turns toward the door when the bell sounds, announcing my entry.

"Mommy!"

I bend down and she runs into my arms. I squeeze her so tightly, sprinkling her face with kisses. "Oh, I missed you so much."

"Me too!"

The chime on the door rings again and Jolie peers over my shoulder, dislodges herself from me, and runs to Jax. He picks her up in one giant swoop, tossing her in the air before situating her on his hip.

Man, he looks good with her. It's like dad crack and I'm a certified addict. I sit on the floor, taking in the sight of the two of them together. She tells him how Gumdrop almost laid down for her and how Dylan's been helping her with him. Jax is just as enthralled by the conversation as she is.

"Want your gifts?" he asks her.

She wiggles to get free and he lets her down, then opens his suitcase since he's the one who had the room to fit a giant M&M dispenser, a *Paw Patrol* stuffed animal, and all the other small things he just had to get her.

"Can we fill it now?" she asks when he hands her the green M&M dispenser.

"Yeah," Jax says at the same time I say no.

I change my mind. "Sure."

They both sit in the waiting room, him showing her how it works, and I head over to my station, wheeling my bag behind me.

"So how was it?" Dylan asks. "You going to go on the road?"

His tone says he's joking, but I'm sure it's something Dylan fears. It wasn't that long ago that Ink Envy was suffering. Jax coming here saved it, and if Jax decides to leave, that would probably cause a huge rift between them.

"I'm happy here." I sit down and put all my things back at my station. "This is where I belong."

"It's good to hear that." Dylan smiles at me. "I was just showing Jolie your picture on Instagram. From what I see, you guys rocked it."

My gaze falls to Jax as he looks at me and says, "She did. Don't be surprised if you get some calls coming in for her. She's going to be fully booked soon."

"Good," Dylan says. "And how about you? Miss it?"

Jax shrugs and Jolie puts her hands on his face, turning him to pay attention to her. After they fill the dispenser and get the M&M's to come out, Jax returns his attention to Dylan. "Not one bit."

Dylan's shoulders release the tension he must have felt from both of us leaving to do a pop-up. With Jax's reputation of running away, I think Dylan was more scared than he let on.

"Want to take Gumdrop for a walk?" Jax asks Jolie, and she jumps up.

"She's been cooped up in here all afternoon," Dylan says.

Jax grabs her jacket off the coat hook and holds it out for her. "We'll be back," he tells me, and he holds the leash until they get on the sidewalk.

"So?" Dylan asks.

I turn in my chair to face him and pull my legs up to my chest. "What?"

"Things going well?"

I nod.

"You have that look on your face." He points at me as if I haven't looked in the mirror since last night.

It might sound funny, but Dylan's like the brother I never had. He knows things about me that I've never felt comfortable telling other people. He's been there for me more than once in my life. So I know what he's really asking.

"We're together and it feels really good."

He smiles, but it doesn't reach his eyes. "It looks good on you, but—"

I put up my hand. "I know you have a history with him. But we talked a lot on this trip, and I think you're underestimating your friend."

"I'm not underestimating him." Dylan looks at Lyle at the front desk. "Hey, Lyle, can you count inventory for me? I have to do an order."

Lyle hops down from his perch and I sigh, knowing Dylan is about to give me some fatherly lecture.

Once Lyle disappears into the back, Dylan starts in. "I love Jax like a brother, but because I'm as close to him as a brother, I see his faults too. He's a great guy, one I'd choose to have on my side all the time. But he's got wounds, cuts so deep I'm not sure they'll ever properly heal. I hope one day he wakes up and flushes out all that shit from childhood, but I also know he was dealt the shittiest hand a foster kid can get."

"Dylan—"

He doesn't let me continue. "I see the way you look at him, and Jolie too. And you've both been hurt so much, I'd feel horrible if it happens again. Just be cautious, okay? Slow it down a little. You guys are moving so fast, and if I've learned anything from my time with Jax, it's that fast scares him."

I walk over and hug him. "That's for your concern. But I'm a big girl and I can handle myself. I trust him."

His eyes are wide. "You do?"

I nod. Maybe not fully until last night, but Jax's ability to open up to me felt so much bigger than anything else. "I do."

"Okay then." Dylan picks up his laptop and buries his head in it as though he's okay, but I wonder when the thought that Jax is going to break me won't be something that burdens him.

A LITTLE OVER A WEEK LATER, I walk into Sweet Infusion because Rian is having a big Valentine's Day baking party where kids can drop in and decorate a heart-shaped cookie for free. Jolie's been begging me to do it, and since I have a little time between clients, I decided now was the perfect opportunity.

She and I sit at a table with two other girls and their moms. The dads are along the wall, talking sports.

Kamea comes over and hands us a decorating tray. "It's

crazy in here." We both look at Rian behind the counter, wiping her forehead with her sleeve. "She's a bit stressed. But the turnout has been great, and people are buying, so it's all good."

Kamea bends down and explains everything to Jolie before running over to some new people who have just come into the shop.

The moms across the table smile at me, but they continue to talk about their plans for the big night. Sounds like each couple is going out for Valentine's Day tonight even though it's tomorrow.

"What do you think, Mommy, pink or purple?" Jolie holds up the icing packets.

"You do what you want, kiddo."

She picks purple—which I could have told her she would since it's her favorite color. She licks the frosting off her fingers while she decorates the cookie, and more of the candies find their way into her belly than onto the cookie, but I decided a long time ago to pick my battles and this isn't one worth fighting.

Jax was right, I've been booked up since the pop-up, and Jolie is the one suffering. My mommy guilt is huge.

Rian gets a break and comes over, pulling up a chair. "Hey, Jolie, I love your cookie." Her hand runs down my arm. "How are things? Dylan said you're killing it."

I notice the stares of the moms on the other side of the large table. "It's been busy, yeah."

"That's awesome. Dylan would never tell you, but he was worried you'd love it and you two would go out on the road."

I laugh. "With Jolie?"

"He had this whole vision of the three of you traveling the world." She laughs.

I knew he was worried. "Yeah, because I seem like a homeschool mom, right?"

We both laugh this time. I'd be tattooing and asking Jolie to repeat the alphabet to me.

"I told him that Jax already lived that life and there's a reason he came back. And that you're a mom before you're a tattoo artist."

I run my hand down Jolie's hair. "That's the truth."

"Rian!" Kamea calls from across the room.

Rian stands. "We really need to have a girls' night soon, because I need some details on what exactly is going on with you two." She waggles her eyebrows.

"Definitely."

Jolie finishes her cookie, and I'm about to tell her we need to go when the little girls across from us color on the sheets in the middle of the table with the crayons Rian's provided. Jolie asks if she can color too.

"I have to get going. Can we take it next door?" I ask her.

Jolie shakes her head. I can tell she wants to interact with the girls across from her, because her eyes keep shifting in that direction.

"Rich, I want to go down to that wine store down the block. Can you sit with her?" the one mom asks and stands, allowing her husband to take her place.

The other husband takes his wife's spot too and the women leave, laughing and smiling as they go.

"Hi," the one dad says to me.

"Hi."

"I like your cookie," he says to Jolie. "I mean the decorating you did... never mind."

We both laugh, and Jolie's small forehead crinkles.

His face grows red and his friend rolls his eyes. "Nothing good comes from that sentence."

"Sorry." The dad shakes his head at me.

I wave him off. "It's okay. I know what you meant."

The girls continue to color, and the dad named Rich leans forward. "Have you been here before?"

At first, I don't realize he's talking to me, but I look up and he's waiting for my answer.

"Yes, my good friend owns it." I point out Rian.

He nods. "We're from Peekskil. My wife wanted to do something with our daughter before we disappear into the city for Valentine's Day."

"It's a great place. She's really good with kids."

Jolie glances up from coloring, so I know she's listening.

"This is a great idea. God knows my wife will buy a dozen of something before we leave," the other guy says. "I'd rather hang out at the tattoo place next door though."

Jolie picks her head up. I wish I could cover her mouth, but that would be rude. I'm not surprised when she says, "That's where my mommy works."

"Really?" Rich asks, his gaze falling down my body as though he could see my tattoos under my jacket and jeans.

I check my watch because my client will be there in a minute. "Yeah."

The door opens, and I'm relieved to see Jax walk through. He smiles and winds his way through the room, seemingly having no idea that every woman in the room has taken more than a glance at him. The moms watch intently as he slides through tables until he reaches us.

"Hey, I just finished. Your client is due in now, right?" Jax glances at the clock on the wall.

I stand and he puts his arm around me, kissing me before sitting down in my place. We've shown a little more affection in front of Jolie, but still sleep in separate bedrooms. But we need to have a discussion with Jolie—soon.

Jax puts his arm around Jolie. "Where's my cookie?"

Jolie laughs. "You have to make one."

He puts his arm around my waist, patting my ass. Luckily, I'm facing the wall. "You go. I got this."

Rian comes over and hands Jax a tray. "I figured you're one of the kids," she says with a sweet smile.

I chuckle.

"Funny, Rian. I would love to decorate a cookie. Usually I only like to decorate Frankie's but…"

"Mommy doesn't bake," Jolie says as if Jax is crazy.

The entire table laughs, even the dads across the way, the one dad nodding at Jax for a good joke. The three little girls are talking, which is nice since Jolie is always around adults. First, they ask for specific colors of crayons, then they compliment one another on their drawings.

Dylan walks in. "Full house," he says to Rian and kisses her. He bends down and kisses Jolie's head. "Awesome job."

The dads are looking at us, probably thinking we're a blended family, but none of them ask. I should've known it would be the little girls who would.

"Who is that?" the one girl asks, pointing at Dylan.

"My uncle Dylan," Jolie answers.

"And who is he?" the other one asks, pointing at Jax.

"That's my daddy…" Jolie pauses. "I mean, Jax."

Jax freezes and frosting drips all over his cookie. Rian grips my forearm as if I don't know what a pivotal moment this is. My heart has literally stopped.

"Is that like a stepdad?" the one girl asks.

"What's a Jax?" the other girl asks.

Jolie shakes her head and doesn't look up. "He's just Jax."

Jax slowly sets down the cookie stuff, and when he rises from the chair, dread fills my veins, weighing me down and keeping me in place.

"Hey," Dylan says to him.

Jax grips my waist and places a quick kiss on my lips. "I'm

sorry... I just need to... I have to go." But he stops and kisses Jolie's head. "See you later. I forgot I have an appointment."

"Jax," Dylan calls.

But we all watch Jax leave the store. After the door shuts, Dylan looks at me. But all I can process is Jax's apology. What is he apologizing for?

CHAPTER TWENTY-NINE

Jax

*M*y phone rings in my pocket, and I pull it out, seeing Holder's name on the screen.

"Hey," I say.

"I found your aunt and she's willing to talk to you."

I sit on a bench on the side of the road. What perfect fucking time. A reminder that I was given up before I could rely on anyone.

"Yeah?" I can't manage to inject any enthusiasm into my voice.

"I thought you'd be more excited. I'm emailing you all her information. But there's something you need to know."

"What's that?" I lean forward and put my head in my palm.

"She didn't know about you. She didn't know you existed."

"Great."

"But she does have an idea of who your dad might've been. I'm having my investigator look into it now. I'll let you know what I find out."

I nod.

"Jax?"

"I'm here."

"Give her a call. She was excited to find out about you. I think it's a good first step."

I ask, "Where does she live?"

"In your old neighborhood."

My heart squeezes. Could I know the woman? "Icing on the cake."

"Listen, I'll let you go ahead and contact her while I try to find out about your dad. Sound good?"

I nod again before realizing he can't see me. "Yeah, sure."

"And please tell Frankie that you paid her lawyer's bill. I'm surprised she hasn't taken her business elsewhere thinking I can't track my financials. She gave me another check a few weeks ago."

I laugh because of course she did. "Okay, I will."

"Good. This is all great news. Be happy."

"Thanks a lot."

"It's what you paid me to do. Bye, Jax."

The call ends, and I hold the phone as I lean forward on the park bench. Just a week ago, I felt as if such a weight had been lifted off me after Frankie and I hashed out what we wanted. But hearing Jolie call me Daddy then retract it so fast sent me into a tailspin.

I pick up the phone and dial her.

"Hey," Frankie answers. I hear it in her tone—she's unsure where we stand.

"I know you're with a client right now, but I wanted to say that I'm sorry for running out. It's just... a lot."

She covers the receiver and tells her client she'll be right back. "I know. I wish she could understand, but she's only five, Jax."

"Holder found my aunt," I say, changing the subject. "I'm going to head over there now."

"Oh, that's great. Do you want me to go with you?"

"No, I just need some time, but I don't want you to get the wrong idea either. So I just wanted to call."

"Okay." There's uncertainty in her voice, but I can't blame her.

"We're good," I try to reassure her, but the truth is that I'm sinking into a bubble of doubt that I'll fail that little girl.

"Okay."

"I'll be home tonight," I say, standing from the bench, needing to move.

"Okay."

I hate that I'm doing this to her, but I have to get my head straight before I enter that apartment again. Jolie deserves a man who is going to step up. I refused the role once already. I can't do it again.

"Text me if you need me," I say, about to hang up.

"Okay. Jax?"

"Yeah?"

"I hope you get the answers you want. I really do."

"Thanks, Frankie."

I hang up and pull up the email from Holder. There's her name, Margaret Nettlebaum, in black font. I'm not sure I want to speak to her, but I head to the train station and buy a ticket to the old neighborhood.

As the train whizzes by, I can't get Jolie's face out of my head. The way she never looked up at me after she said daddy. The smile I've become addicted to fading as she said, "Just Jax." I don't want to be a stepdad or just Jax, but daddy comes with a level of responsibility I've never considered for myself.

The train stops and I get off. She lives on the other side of town in a small apartment complex with a garden next door and a park across the street. I sit on a park bench and stare at the complex. Dead flower beds hang from the windows. Everything is clean and kept up fairly well. Valentine's stickers decorate the windows of what I think is her apartment.

I sit and stare for a half hour before a woman walks down the street with a man and two boys. The man checks me out, probably thinking I'm a threat, so I pull out my phone as though I have something to do and I'm not a creep with no children, sitting in a park.

The man places his hand on the small of the woman's back and ushers the two boys up the stairs. I glance up from my phone as they open the apartment door and take the stairs. The lights turn on in the third-floor apartment with the heart stickers on the windows. The woman walks by the window, stops and looks out, but turns away before making eye contact with me.

I stand, not wanting to scare her and figuring I'll head to Mama Whelan's to get my head on straight. She's always been Team Jax, even when I did stupid shit like sleep with Dylan's girl.

As I round the park, someone calls, "Excuse me?"

I turn to find the woman behind me. She stops and tightens her cardigan sweater around her middle. The man is waiting on the stairs. I don't say anything and her breath catches.

"Are you him? Jax? Jax Owens?"

I nod.

A huge smile wraps around her mouth and her shoulders fall. She turns around and nods to her husband, but he doesn't move. "I thought so. I talked with a Mr. Holder earlier today. I was hoping you'd reach out."

"Really?"

She remains on the corner of the park. Neither of us walks toward the other, as though both of our feet are stuck in cement. She nods. "You have her eyes."

I nod, unable to find any words. I've never heard anything like that in my entire life.

She glances over her shoulder again at her husband. "Would you like to come up? We're just making Valentines and eating junk food. Kind of a tradition for us."

I shake my head. "I don't want to impose."

"Nonsense. Come on." She nods toward the stairs. I step forward, and she waits to walk with me. "I'm Maggie, by the way." She looks at me. "You're tall."

She's very petite. I wonder if my mom was too.

We walk across the street. "This is my husband, Pete."

He puts his hand out with a welcoming smile. "Nice to meet you."

"Jax," I say.

He nods as though he knows and opens the apartment door, allowing Maggie and me to go through first. We walk up the stairs. When we reach their door, the whole outside is decorated in red and pink heart garland. A sign on the door says, "Take one," with a pocket where boxes of conversation heart candies sit.

"You really like Valentine's Day, huh?"

Pete laughs behind me. "More than you know. I keep telling her that I'll take her out for the night, get a sitter, but she says all three of us are her Valentines."

We walk in, and two boys are sitting at a table with glitter, glue, and construction paper.

"Boys, this is Jax. Jax, this is Will and Sam."

They both say hi, and I say hi back.

Pete slaps me on the back. "Can I get you a drink?"

"Um... a water?"

"Coming right up." He walks by me and goes to the kitchen, returning with a water for me and a glass of wine for Maggie. "If you need something stronger, just let me know."

"This is good, thanks." I hold up the water bottle.

"We'll be in here if you need us." He kisses his wife's cheek and sits at the table with his boys.

Maggie holds her arm out toward the family room. "Want to sit?"

"Sure." I remove my jacket and sit on the couch. There's a box of pictures on the coffee table, a few stacks looking like someone's been going through them.

Maggie sits next to me and picks up a picture. "I'm not sure you're ready, but I'm a firm believer in taking a sledge-hammer to break the ice." She hands me a picture. "This is your mom, or was."

I stare at the picture of a woman who, as Maggie said, has the same eyes as me. Not just the color, but the shape and deeper set too.

I hand it back to her, but she holds up her hand. "No, that's yours to keep. I was looking through these earlier in case you reached out."

She hands me a stack. I place my water bottle down and flip through them.

"I was a lot younger than Tina, so a lot was kept from me. And until Mr. Holder called, I had no idea she was ever pregnant. She died of an overdose. My parents kicked her out after she finished high school because she was stealing and using and hanging around bad people. I'm not sure my parents ever knew she was pregnant either. I think if they had, they would've taken you in. At least I like to think they would."

"Are they alive?"

She gives me a sad smile. "My mom is alive. She's in a nursing home. Sadly, Dad passed."

"What happened to him?"

She picks up a picture and shows me a fairly recent one of a man on a plaid couch. "He just never took care of himself, never went to the doctor. They say it was natural causes." She shrugs. "I'm really sorry, Jax." She sips her wine. "Did you have a family who adopted you? Mr. Holder wasn't very forthcoming with any details about your life."

I shake my head and place the pictures down. "No. I grew up in the system."

Her hand touches my arm. "Oh no. I'm so sorry."

I shrug. "It's okay. You didn't leave me there."

She's quiet for a moment. "She wouldn't have been a good mother. I know that's bad to say as her sister, and probably doesn't give you much comfort, but it's true. She couldn't even take care of herself. She probably thought leaving you was the best choice. It's the most selfless thing I ever knew her to do."

I never really thought about that. That maybe she hoped I'd have a better life than I did.

"But I wish we would have known. I really do."

"Thanks." I stand.

"You don't have to leave. I'd love to learn more about you." She looks me over. "You like tattoos, huh?"

"Holder said something about you thinking you might know who my dad is?"

"I thought I might, but looking at you... you're so tall and good-looking. I'm not sure the guy I thought of is your dad. He had red hair and was fair-skinned." I sit again, and she stands. "Let me get something for you to take those pictures with you."

She leaves and returns with an envelope, then shoves

pictures I don't really want in there. But I guess I should keep them to show my kids one day, if I have any.

"I was hoping you could maybe fill in some blanks for my medical history... at least on my mom's side. Is there anything that runs in the family? What boxes should I be checking next time I fill out a form at the doctor's?" I give her a half-smile.

She taps her pointer finger on her lips like she's thinking about it for a moment. "I know high blood pressure was an issue on my dad's side and a few people on my mom's side developed diabetes as they got older, but as far as I know there's no type of cancer or anything that's been a real issue."

Well, at least there's that. "Great, thanks for the info." I stand, ready to leave, and she walks me to the door. We exchange numbers, although I'm not sure I'll ever use hers. We say an awkward goodbye, both unsure if we should hug or not.

I'm walking down the stairs, not feeling complete like I thought I would. I thought meeting a blood family member would change me.

I'm on the landing of the second floor when she rushes out of her apartment and leans over the railing. "Jax?"

I look up.

"Can I ask you a question?"

I walk up a few steps to get closer. "Sure."

"Are you happy? I know how you grew up was probably a nightmare, but now that you're an adult. Did you find happiness?" A tear slips down her cheek, but she quickly brushes it away with the back of her hand.

I think for a moment. Frankie comes to mind, Jolie right after. Dylan and Rian, Knox, as well as all the true friendships I've made since returning to Cliffton Heights. "Yeah. I am."

She smiles, which I return. I walk down the stairs at peace

with my answer. I am happy. I can't think of a time I've ever been happier.

Now it's time to tell the ones who are responsible for that happiness.

CHAPTER THIRTY

Frankie

Since Jolie nodded off in her bedroom while reading a book, I use the opportunity to clean up her toys strewn around the apartment. I'm almost done when I hear arguing in the hallway. I open the door and find Jax there with Dylan.

"Where the hell did you go?" Dylan yells.

"It's none of your business," Jax says.

"Come on, you two." Rian pulls Dylan away.

Jax glances over, spotting me in the doorway. He smiles and breezes by Dylan. "Hey."

"Hey," I say.

I tried to act strong. I wanted to give Jax the benefit of the doubt. Jolie calling him daddy wasn't exactly an easy thing to swallow. Especially with his self-doubt about being someone who can be relied on as heavily as a child does a parent.

"Jax, if you fuck this up—" Dylan starts.

Jax raises his hand and turns around. "I love you, man. You're my brother. And I know I did you wrong once, and I ran away. You think I'm more screwed up in the head than you, but truth is, my head's screwed on pretty straight— now." He glances at me over his shoulder. "I know that you being a dick is just your way of preparing yourself for the chance I run again. You're trying to protect not just Frankie and Jolie, but yourself." He hugs Dylan and pats him on the back. "But I'm not going anywhere. In fact, thanks. If you wouldn't have allowed me to rent a chair at Ink Envy, I never would have met Frankie."

Jax releases Dylan, and Rian looks at them with that look she gets when she loves something. It is kind of funny to see Jax so happy and open with his feelings.

"Now, if you'll excuse me, I have to plan a big event," Jax says. "It's not every day you ask someone if you can be their daddy."

Jax picks up two bags from the floor, kisses me on the lips, and walks into the apartment.

"Do you think he's high?" Rian asks. "I mean, I've never seen him like this."

Dylan shakes his head at me with a smile. "Come on, Rian, time for us to stay out of their business. Jax is all grown up now."

I laugh and turn around, walking inside the apartment and shutting the door. "Hey."

Jax is taking a bunch of Valentine decorations out of the bags, but he stops and comes over to me. "I'm sorry if I scared you. It cut me the way she was so sad when she corrected those girls and said I'm just Jax. I've been screwed up, but I'm not anymore. I want this. I want you and Jolie. I want us to be a family."

He pulls me into a hug, and I stand stiffly, unsure of who this man is. "Okay."

Then he continues taking the decorations out of the bag. He picks up an envelope and hands it to me. "Maybe keep those safe. We can show our kids one day."

I open the envelope and see pictures of a woman who has the same eyes as Jax. Then I realize what he said. "Kids?"

He looks up and must realize how thrown off-kilter I am by his new attitude. Taking my hand, he leads me to the couch. "I'm done with all the shit from my past weighing me down. I'm happy. And I'm happy because of you and Jolie. And I know if I fuck up, you'll straighten me out. But I don't think I will because I'm doing a good job now, right? Besides the fuckup today with the daddy thing."

"Jax, are you sure?" I need to make sure he's not just on some high after finally meeting someone genetically related to him.

He takes my face in his hands like he does when he wants me to really hear him. "Positive. I've been ridiculous, thinking that because my mom didn't want me, no one ever would. That just because I didn't have a father figure, I didn't know how to be one. But that's not true."

I shake my head, tears welling. He finally sees what I see. "No, it's not."

He presses his lips to mine. "I love you, Frankie."

I blink in surprise.

"I wanted to say it that night in Vegas, but I was chicken-shit. And you don't have to say it back to me. If you don't love me yet, it's okay. I'll make sure you will." He smiles and kisses me again.

"I do love you. I just didn't want to scare you." God, it feels so good to let those words loose into the world.

He smiles. "I'm done being scared."

"Good."

"Want to help me?" he asks, standing and pulling more stuff out of the bag.

"What is all this?"

"Valentine's Day. I've never celebrated it, and this year I have two valentines, you and Jolie." He kisses me again. "The loves of my life."

His happiness is contagious. I can't stop smiling as he hangs streamers and heart-shaped garland around the apartment.

"Oh, and just so you know," Jax says. "I paid Holder your lawyer's fees."

I stomp my foot. "I knew something was up. I was scared he was flighty or something. Thank you, but you cannot keep saving me."

He rounds the counter and pulls me flush against his chest. "Sure, I can. I'm your man."

"For a second I thought you were going to say prince."

He laughs. "Nah, you don't need some prince saving you. You just need someone to stand hand in hand with you as you journey through life. And I couldn't be happier to be the man you chose."

More tears well in my eyes. "I love you."

"I love you." He seals that promise with a kiss.

CHAPTER THIRTY-ONE

Jax

I walk in the door from walking Gumdrop and picking up the last thing I need for this morning. I'm taking off my jacket and unhooking Gumdrop from his leash when Jolie's bedroom door opens. She's in her night-gown and flannel pants, one sock missing. She walks past most of the decorations and sits on the couch, grabbing the remote.

"Jolie," I say, but she lies down on the couch, obviously still tired. I walk over to her and sit down, and she snuggles up on my lap. "Happy Valentine's Day."

Frankie must hear us because she walks out. Jolie peeks up, seeing Frankie coming out of my room.

"Mommy, did you sleep in Jax's room?" she asks, sounding confused.

She's way too observant for her own good.

Frankie sits in the chair across from us. We had a long conversation last night about how we hoped this would go.

"I did," she says.

Jolie sits up and looks at me. "Did you sleep in Mommy's bed? I want to switch beds with someone tonight."

"Not a chance. You'll be in your own bed until you're thirty," I say.

Frankie rolls her eyes, but her smile says she likes me being protective of Jolie. "We need to talk to you about some changes that are happening around here."

Jolie looks at me. She's too smart for her own good too. "What?"

"Jax and Mommy are a couple now. And couples sleep in the same bed. Sometimes they kiss. Sometimes they hug. All because they love one another."

Jolie looks from Frankie to me again. "You love Mommy?"

I nod. "I do."

"And you love Jax?" she asks Frankie.

Frankie giggles. "I do."

"Okay." She crawls off the couch, and it's as though she sees the decorations for the first time. "Whoa."

"Happy Valentine's Day," I say again.

"Happy Valentine's Day." Jolie smiles wide.

"I picked up breakfast." I stand and grab the box I picked up.

Frankie stays on the couch as Jolie climbs up on the breakfast stool.

"Can I talk to you about yesterday?" I whisper.

Jolie's excitement fades. "I'm sorry. I was gonna lie because those girls had their dads, but don't worry. I told them you were just Jax."

I nod, my heart squeezing. "I have something really serious to talk to you about."

"What?" She looks as if she might cry. Maybe she thinks she's in trouble or something. I can't do this to a little girl.

"Open the box." I push it toward her, and Frankie comes up behind her.

Inside the box are conversation heart cookies. Thank you, Rian, for making them, but I've written on each one.

"On Valentine's Day, a lot of people ask other people to be their Valentine. I asked Mommy last night and she said yes. So..." I take out the cookies, move the box, and position them in front of Jolie, pointing at the first one. "Will you.

"Be my.

"Valentine?"

She nods and smiles. "Yes."

"Wait, there's one more cookie, because you have to sign your Valentine, so people know who it's from. You don't want to say yes if you don't like the person."

She nods and looks at my hands.

I place the final cookie in front of her.

"Daddy," she reads before I can say it. Her eyebrows scrunch together.

"I love you, Jolie, and I'd be honored to be your other daddy, if you'll have me."

I can't replace Michael, and I won't try. Maybe he'll end up back in her life if he can get his shit together, and maybe not. But either way, Jolie will always have one daddy who will have her back no matter what.

She looks to Frankie for confirmation that she understands. Frankie nods, looking as if she might burst out in happy tears.

Jolie crawls over the counter and wraps her hands around my neck. "You love me?"

I nod, fighting back the tears.

"Mommy loves me. You love me. I love you. I love Mommy. So can I sleep in your bed too?" she asks.

Frankie laughs, and I open my arms for her to join our hug. Jolie puts one arm around Frankie's neck and one across mine until all our foreheads are touching.

It took me a long-ass time to get here, but this feeling is worth risking everything for.

EPILOGUE

Jax

A year later...

rankie's on my table. It's the first time she's allowed me to ink her, but it won't be the last. I can promise her that.

Jolie sits on a waiting room chair, staring over the half wall. "Why can't I get one?"

Frankie turns toward her and I look up, both of us saying in unison, "When you're eighteen."

She blows out a breath.

"This is taking longer than our wedding ceremony," Ethan says from the waiting area, his hand on Blanca's swollen stomach.

All of our friends watch as I tattoo a wedding band on Frankie's finger.

"At least we're not listening to a one hour mass." Seth sits on the counter in the front.

I finish the tattoo and Frankie raises her hand to look at it. "I was honestly worried you were going to do something obnoxious." She sits up, and I kiss her.

"I probably sketched it out a hundred times." I inspect it to make sure I'm happy with it.

"It's perfect." She puts her arm around my neck. After we kiss again, she hugs me. "It's your turn, big guy."

"First I have a present for you."

"A present?"

Our friends grow disinterested in our way of celebrating our recent courthouse marriage.

I pull out the last "I got Inked by Jax" shirt that Kamea had made for me and hold it out for Frankie. "You have to wear it now."

She laughs and puts it right over her very unique wedding dress. A simple white silk dress that clings to every curve but dips low in the back to show off her ink. And yes, I even wore a suit because we have to have pictures for our kids to look at later.

She jumps off my table and walks over to hers, then pats the bench. "Your turn."

Everyone laughs. Frankie's mad talented too.

"No looking until I'm done," she says.

"Deal." I get on the table and turn away and look at the group of our friends.

I'm not sure how long we'll live in the Rooftop Apartments, but it's a special place where I'd like to think we all found ourselves. Blanca's ready to pop, Sierra and Adrian are two months from their wedding in Sandsal, and though they're hiding it, I know Rian is pregnant. She and Dylan eloped six months ago after issues with her parents around the wedding, and she's been wearing baggy clothes for weeks now. They'll tell us when they're ready.

Seth and Evan are getting married this summer, then they're going on their honeymoon in Europe so Seth can photograph the landscape. Knox told me last night that he's proposing to Kamea in the upcoming weeks.

We've all found our own happily ever afters, and though I never believed it was possible, waking up next to the woman currently inflicting me with pain is the best thing I could ever imagine. We explained to Jolie that she couldn't sleep with us every night, but we let her sneak in on nights when she's scared.

And now that we're married, I think I'm ready for another kid or two. No way Jolie can be an only child. She's already spoiled by all her aunts and uncles.

Sandy stares at us. She sat me down shortly after Frankie and I made our relationship public. Thankfully, Sandy was happy that I could step into a role her son was incapable of filling. She thanked me for taking on the family and protecting Frankie and Jolie. She's still our biggest helper, and she's kind of like a mother to both of us.

Michael hasn't returned since she gave him money and he signed the paperwork giving Frankie sole custody.

My gaze falls to Jolie, and I wink. She smiles, but then Frankie's cousin Aiden picks her up and throws her in the air. Jolie's more enamored by the woman he brought with him.

"All done." Frankie takes off her gloves.

I inspect the F in the center with her signature holistic style, surprised by how masculine she was able to make it, but still let it represent her.

"I love it." And I mean it.

I hop off her table, ready to start the party to celebrate the fact that I married the love of my life, but she stops me with her hand on my arm. "I got a present for you too."

"You did?"

She pulls something from her drawer. A black T-shirt. She holds it up for me. "I'd Rather Be Getting Inked By Frankie."

I look back at Kamea and she hides behind Knox. Stepping forward, I take my new wife by the waist. "That better be a one-off."

"I guess you'll find out." She leans back and pulls the T-shirt over my head.

"Perfect fit," I say.

"Yep. So that's it? You're mine?" she asks.

"Appears so. What do you want to do now, Mrs. Owens?"

She pretends to think about it. "Live happily ever after?"

I chuckle. "You married Jax Owens. That's a given."

She rolls her eyes like she has since the first time I met her, but I dip her and kiss the living crap out of her while our friends hoot and holler. I stand Frankie back up and look at her and Jolie and all of our friends. Sometimes family is the people you choose. I sure as hell chose right.

The End

COCKAMAMIE UNICORN RAMBLINGS

It's sad to see the Rooftop Crew go. We fell in love with this group hard. Maybe because their characters were a little more broken than we usually write in our romcoms. Dylan and Jax being foster kids was a hard topic to tackle. Add on Frankie being in a relationship with a man who is not only addicted but has been physically abusive? Rom com gold right? Not. And that's not even mentioning little Jolie who just wants a daddy to help raise her.

As most of you unicorns have probably clued in on, we decide on titles before we ever plot the book. And if you've read our ramblings before, you know that we've written ourselves into a corner numerous times. But A Co-Workers Crush was a nice change because we were able to tease it from the get go. Although we didn't know about Jax until the end of book two, we did plan for Frankie to be the girl in this book. Thank goodness for the writing gods who brought Jax on the page because we can't think of anyone better suited for Frankie.

There isn't much that changed in this book after we plotted from to when we were writing, except that Jax wasn't going to search out his birth parents at all but we felt it was his character arc, to find the closure from his past to set forth into the future. Michael wasn't going to play such a major role in the story, he was going to be long gone the entire book, but then we had him around more than anticipated because that's not always real life. Real life is messy.

We hope you enjoyed the uniqueness of each couple we wrote in this series. Each one brought something different as far as their wound of why they couldn't love. And that is what we strive to bring you—different journeys with a variety of heroes and heroines.

Now let's all go to the rooftop and have a drink with them! Cheers.

Once again, thank you to our tremendous team!

Danielle Sanchez and the entire Wildfire Marketing Solutions team.

Cassie from Joy Editing for line edits.

Ellie from My Brother's Editor for line edits.

Shawna from Behind the Writer for proofreading.

Hang Le for the cover and branding for the entire series.

Wander Aguiar for the amazing photo of Frankie and Jax.

Bloggers who consistently carve out time to read, review and/or promote us.

Piper Rayne Unicorns who shout from the rooftops about our new releases and love our characters like we do.

Readers who took a chance on our book with so many choices out there.

Aiden, our Lucky #13, is first up in the Hockey Hotties series and was originally just going to be a guy who came into Ink

Envy for a tattoo. BUT... making him Frankie's cousin was so much better. His series will be coming in June 2021 and there will definitely be some cameos of the Rooftop Crew.

XO,
    Piper & Rayne

ABOUT THE AUTHOR

Piper Rayne is a USA Today Bestselling Author duo who write "heartwarming humor with a side of sizzle" about families, whether that be blood or found. They both have e-readers full of one-clickable books, they're married to husbands who drive them to drink, and they're both chauffeurs to their kids. Most of all, they love hot heroes and quirky heroines who make them laugh, and they hope you do, too!

ALSO BY PIPER RAYNE

The Rooftop Crew

My Bestie's Ex

A Royal Mistake

The Rival Roomies

Our Star-Crossed Kiss

The Do-Over

A Co-Workers Crush

Hockey Hotties

My Lucky #13

The Trouble with #9

Faking it with #41

The Baileys

Lessons from a One-Night Stand

Advice from a Jilted Bride

Birth of a Baby Daddy

Operation Bailey Wedding (Novella)

Falling for My Brother's Best Friend

Demise of a Self-Centered Playboy

Confessions of a Naughty Nanny

Operation Bailey Babies (Novella)

Secrets of the World's Worst Matchmaker

Winning My Best Friend's Girl

Rules for Dating your Ex

Operation Bailey Birthday (Novella)

The Greenes

My Beautiful Neighbor

My Almost Ex

My Vegas Groom

The Modern Love World

Charmed by the Bartender

Hooked by the Boxer

Mad about the Banker

The Single Dad's Club

Real Deal

Dirty Talker

Sexy Beast

Hollywood Hearts

Mister Mom

Animal Attraction

Domestic Bliss

Bedroom Games

Cold as Ice

On Thin Ice

Break the Ice

Box Set

Charity Case

Manic Monday

Afternoon Delight

Happy Hour

Blue Collar Brothers

Flirting with Fire

Crushing on the Cop

Engaged to the EMT

White Collar Brothers

Sexy Filthy Boss

Dirty Flirty Enemy

Wild Steamy Hook-up